BODYPOWER!

by Marylou McKenna

Photographs by Sheldon Segunda

Simon and Schuster   New York

Designed by Jill Weber
Manufactured in the United States of America

1 2 3 4 5 6 7 8 9 10

LIBRARY OF CONGRESS CATALOGING IN PUBLICATION DATA

McKenna, Marylou.
   Bodypower!.

   Bibliography: p.
   Includes index.
   1. Women—Health and hygiene. 2. Women—Psychology. 3. Exercise
for women. 4. Stress (Physiology) I. Title.
RA778.M148   613′.04′244   75–45361
ISBN 0–671–22217–1

Acknowledgments

For manuscript readings and other professional encouragement I would like to thank Dr. Joseph A. Bailey, Dr. Philip Casson, Dr. Emanuel M. Greenberg, Dr. Hans Kraus, and Dr. Hans Selye. Librarians at the New York Academy of Medicine were of invaluable aid, as were members of the New York Academy of Science.

For the chapter on stress I am indebted to Dr. Thomas Holmes and Dr. Minoru Masuda of the University of Washington, who were the first to chart the biological impact of life changes today and relate these stressors to mind and body breakdowns.

For advice and expert direction for the chapters on emotionality and the psychophysical techniques, I thank Dr. Alexander Lowen, distinguished pioneer in the new field of body/ mind (and less pretentious than many lesser lights). Other professionals provided special help, including Miki Kronold and Bill Johnson of the Institute for Bioenergetic Analysis, Ilana Rubenfeld and Inez Zeller of the Alexander movement, and Dr. Ida Rolf and Rose Feitis of the Structural Integration Foundation. Charlotte Selver offered unique insights, as did members of the Association for Humanistic Psychology. And last but never least, my thanks to Will Schutz and staff members at Esalen Institute.

The nutrition chapter and other medical sections benefited from the expertise of Margaret Markham of the Vitamin Information Bureau, Dr. Victoria A. Bradess, and Emily La Pardo of the American Health Foundation, as well as doughty Dr. Max Warmbrand. In Europe, physicians and personnel at Zurich's Bircher-Benner Clinic accorded help beyond the call of courtesy, as did Dr. William Griffith McBride, top gynecologist/scientist whom I interviewed in Sydney, Australia.

Paul Demming and Dr. Vincent E. Price of the Institute for General Medical Studies, National Institutes of Health, in Bethesda, Maryland, were helpful. So were William Beidler of Guilford College, Moshe Davidowitz of New York University, and Dr. B. Man Yoon of Fordham University.

Polly Bergen, Francis Ford Coppola, Joan Crawford, Hildegarde, Hans Holzer, and Dorothy Sarnoff gave me an insider's look at various types of professional stress. Back in New York City, Rosemary Clark of the American Heart Association, George S. Thommen, W. Meade, Roz Targ, George Nicholas, Elizabeth Rich, and Hy Gardner provided tangible aid and welcome support.

Neil Hickey deserves appreciation for his splendid effort as editorial consultant on this definitive undertaking. I also thank Michael Korda (a chivalrous reminder of the gentlemanly era in publishing), who marshaled the Simon and Schuster team and kept things moving.

I thank my parents, William and Mary Tudor, Vivian Rendu, and close friends (you know who you are) who were tolerant of an author who became somewhat intense (and probably a bit of a bore) in this mind-stretching effort to chart new horizons and scale nebulous mountain peaks. And for reinforcement during the long and hectic four years that went into this project, I am grateful to my younger daughter, Kate Dylan. With patience beyond her years, she stood with cool aplomb in the midst of the fray and never lost faith.

This book is dedicated to my younger daughter—
Kate Dylan McKenna, of New York City, U.S.A.
and my granddaughter—
Natacha Ann-Sophie Rendu of Valenton, France.

Contents

9

When repression is crippling,
Self-knowledge is power.

And this secret spake Life herself
unto me.
"Behold," said she, "I am that
which must ever surpass itself.
To be sure, ye call it will to
procreation,
or impulse towards a goal,
towards the higher, remoter,
more manifold;
But all that is one and the same
secret. . . ."
And this heard I secondly: "Whatever
cannot obey itself, is commanded.
Such is the nature of living things."

—*Friedrich Nietzsche*

CHAPTER 1

How to Get the Most
Out of Yourself
(and the Best Out of Life)

An eight months' pregnant woman who could not swim jumped into an ice-encrusted mountain lake and singlehandedly saved her two children from drowning. Much later, when asked about her feat, she appeared somewhat embarrassed. "It was the only thing to do," she said.

In America's Midwest, during a lightning-filled summer storm, a slight, middle-aged woman held up a mangled automobile chassis under which her son was pinned. She stayed calm, encouraging the teenager to lie quietly until a rescue team arrived.

Shipwrecked in the Pacific, a young English bride, delicate and unable to swim, survived for more than four months on a tiny raft with her husband. Buffeted by storms, beset by hunger and thirst, she never lost confidence that searchers would find them. Her husband later said that her cheer kept his spirits up and his hope alive.

These were everyday, ordinary women, none of them athletic or remarkably strong (in fact, two were quite frail). Yet under extraordinary pressures, they were extraordinarily hardy and capable. How could they muster such physical and emotional strengths when there was nothing in their backgrounds to prepare them for such arduous exertion?

17

The answers to this question have traditionally been "we don't know," or "it's a miracle." But today's scientific techniques make possible a new answer which can dramatically change our lives: great powers lie within the reach of every "ordinary" individual. The examples cited here of women finding increased strength during stress situations, along with countless other instances, particularly in wartime, of persons who were not even physically fit, much less strong, showing uncommon stamina, have demonstrated to scientists that *most of us normally exist at only fifteen percent of our physical and emotional capabilities.* The superpowers brought forth in exceptional circumstances are not fantasy; they are part of our everyday potential. And with the help of new psycho-medical techniques, we can all learn to make use of this reserve inner force on a daily basis.

The scientific sophistication that made possible the revolution in space flight is being paralleled today by a revolution of the body. Ninety percent of all the scientists who ever lived are alive and working today, and the true wonder of "space age medicine" is that we are learning how to make the ordinary body achieve exceptional power. Although the psycho-medical advances and techniques we will explore in this book are of importance to both men and women, there is no question but that it is women who will most uniquely benefit from them. The real revolution of our era is a revolution by, for, and about women. The powers of body and mind available to the woman of today promise her a future that is virtually limitless in its possibilities.

The so-called negative qualities that have limited women for centuries—charges of being too "emotional," or "sensitive," or "overreacting"—are now proving to be advantageous. The quick "mind-body" responsiveness that causes "housewife fatigue," a tension-riddled body, and anxious self-doubt can now be used to work *for* women. When a woman learns to control her mind through her body, *and vice versa,* she will discover the thrill and excitement of becoming the person she was meant to be.

Psychologists state that strength of purpose in itself can open the stubborn doors of success. Studies of faith healers, for example, show that a confident attitude* can escalate the individual toward ever higher goals. Therefore, I ask you, the reader, as an experiment, to suspend your conditional skepticism enough to accept the fact that radical changes—what we once called "miracles"—are possible for you too. If you will allow yourself to be receptive, the techniques reported in this book will make astounding and highly satisfying changes in your life. They have in mine. Never an athletic person, I have learned the thrill of opening up, at will, hidden physical and mental powers within myself. You can, also.

One of the most exciting benefits of Bodypower for women is the slowing of the aging process. It is a biological law that what we don't use, we lose. And there is an emotional law as well. This is something the Greeks understood when they defined happiness as using as much of oneself as possible in search of excellence. Unlocking your hidden abilities to achieve this excellence brings to women a singing self-confidence and a higher, more evolved form of self-love. One of the best-kept secrets of the rejuvenation world is that when a person learns to reach inside her psyche and trains her body to burn with the right kind of steady flame, many vital processes become self-renewing. A revitalizing energy is released which produces a glowing, more youthful appearance. This leads into that rewarding, sexy pride that the French describe as *"être bien dans sa peau"* (literally, "to feel good in one's skin"). To awaken each day with a thrill of eager expectancy is what the Good Life is all about; this can be achieved through the techniques of Bodypower.

* The magnetism of a "winner" can be learned, according to psychologist Richard Taylor, who proved that a gambler's runs of luck often result from sheer self-confidence. He asked two groups of people to guess color sequences in a pack of playing cards. Regardless of their choices, he told one group they had done exceptionally well and that they were naturally lucky. In further testing, this group guessed the color sequences with more accuracy than the other. "Luck," this psychologist maintains, "is a state of mind."

NEVER A GREATER NEED

At the beginning of this chapter we told of three women whose miraculous stamina under pressure was a surprise to themselves as well as family and friends. What made their stories newsworthy is a telling indictment of our times. Just as civilization and technological progress have brought social and economic advancement, they have also ushered in physical and emotional debilitation. Despite public health advances and improved nutrition, most women today are less physically fit than their grandmothers and great-grandmothers were at the same age. Life spans have been lengthened, epidemics contained, and many diseases eliminated, but a new "space age fatigue" stems from modern anxieties. It affects even the healthiest women. Chronic tiredness turns women into underachievers. This fact is particularly disturbing in a time when new opportunities for women are opening up all around us.

Contemporary women are expected to cope with a greater variety of stress than any women in history. Although automation has made more leisure time possible, today's woman has had her energies too depleted to enjoy herself with carefree confidence.

Faced as she is with an unrelenting onslaught of TV bombardment (25,000 commercials annually for the occasional television viewer), flashing signs, and hard-sell radio advertising, today's woman is constantly being "urged." She is subjected to more images and subliminal harassments in a single day than her grandmother had to cope with in a month.

Nerves jumping and thoughts distracted, many women suffer from too much "input." Their minds can get out of kilter, like a broken computer tape, at the close of a hectic day. It should be no surprise that these women often become overweight, indecisive and emotionally harried. Filled with self-doubt and easily exasperated, they find themselves robbed of the drive that can convert even limited talent into achievement.

The impact of modern civilization takes a special toll on women's private lives. Population growth may have been slowed, but there are still too many people moving at hectic pace. Super-cities now spread across North America and down both coast-lines. The physically satisfying work-and-rest habits of previous centuries are gone now. Lifestyles have been dramatically altered by recent urbanization and an increasing number of household moves. A woman is nurtured by her home environment. Change her residence, and "transplant trauma" becomes another adaptation demand on an already overburdened body and mind. In big cities women encounter new conflicts and anxieties: hostilities are caused by overcrowding, mass transportation delays and utility breakdowns. There are risks of burglary, murder, muggings, and rape. The daily bombardment of crime reports on radio, television, and in the press does not make it easy to remain emotionally unaffected.

The turmoil and insecurity of contemporary times have forced some women into flight from traditional institutions. Many women feel that conventional marriage can actually restrict their development and intellectual growth. Feeling unfulfilled, unwanted, or simply exasperated, the "runaway wife" is a recent social phenomenon. Emotional and social stress have combined to make a dramatic exit seem easier than trying to tailor a new life out of the shabby remains of old ideas and old habits.

Divorce statistics are at an all-time high, and it is usually the woman who initiates the divorce. Yet, many of these women, discouraged with conventional patterns, are at a loss to explain what they *do* want out of life. But they are sure of one thing: they are eager—and ready—for change. Yet despite the new opportunities for growth brought about by feminism, many housewives are unable to set goals for themselves; by midafternoon they no longer have the energy to consider anything other than coping with the very routines that enslave them. It is one of the ironies of history that at long last new options are being offered to women, yet stress and fatigue have made many too weary to accept them.

Feminism has also brought a new uneasiness to many women. From the underachieving homemaker (now self-conscious because she is "merely" a wife and mother) to that older woman who finds a lack of kinship with, or respect from, her outspoken, militant daughter (thus adding to her mid-life depressions), the women's liberation movement has had its unintended victims. New opportunities are available, but many women do not have the confidence or energy for continuing education, job changes, political activism, consciousness-raising, or even quiet contentment.

SUICIDES AND BODY BREAKDOWNS INCREASING

Civilization has made many encroachments upon women's minds and bodies. Now medical surveys indicate we have become twice as vulnerable to chronic emotional depression as men. This has sent female suicide statistics zooming. Suicide rates of white American women have increased 49 percent in the last twenty years. Black female suicides have skyrocketed an ominous 80 percent.*

Serious body breakdowns among women also have increased significantly, for women's physical and emotional outlooks are inseparably entwined. Of American deaths recorded from stroke in 1969, over 109,000 were female, compared with some 93,000 male deaths. Some experts attribute the increase in strokes and hypertension to the rising number of female cigarette smokers, as well as to stress and the use of oral contraceptives. Statistical incidence for breast and lung cancer in women has also increased, despite improved diagnostic methods. Female diabetics now outnumber males by nearly one third (with an estimated one million diabetic women *undetected*). Rheumatoid arthritis, which strikes 2.3 times more women than men, osteoarthritis, and even gout—previously a "for men only" affliction—are all on the increase among women.

The stay-at-home woman does not escape this rising incidence of female body disorders. So-called "housewife's ulcer" is

---

* Compare this with a 10 percent rise in white male suicides and a 33 percent increase in black male suicides.

on the increase, as are stomach disorders caused by boredom or repressed anger. Equally formidable are the mysterious fatigues now attributed to electromagnetic home appliances, radar ranges, and microwave ovens. Color TV sets have also been under study for excessive release of radiation.

Many convenience appliances that are ballyhooed as making the homemaker's life carefree and full of fun have been found to produce unpleasant side effects: garbage compactors and certain electric dishwashers operate with such grating noises that the whole body—beginning with the neck and shoulder area—becomes tense, very seriously tense. Even the prudent, medically sophisticated homemaker may be subjected to illness and be unaware of its cause. For if her home is located near a heavy-traffic highway, she inhales automotive fumes that make her vulnerable to respiratory disorders and cancer. Even household dust (especially that which is trapped by bedroom carpeting) has been found to provoke bronchial illness!

Sick, nerve-racked, or merely tired, many women have resorted in desperation to folk medicine and herbal remedies. For, more than other leading professions, *the world of organized medicine has fallen short of fulfilling its ethical responsibilities to women.*

OVERCOMING MEDICAL CHAUVINISM

The health-conscious woman is mocked for her desperate reliance on pharmaceuticals and over-the-counter drugs. Yet her belief in a pill for every purpose is encouraged by her family physician. Surveys show that most doctors feel the most satisfactory way of terminating a patient interview is to dash off a prescription. Since her symptoms are carefully noted only when they are recited in a controlled, dispassionate manner, the emotional (or sick!) woman is victimized by unconscious male medical chauvinism. It springs from three serious failings in contemporary medicine: (1) post-Victorian ignorance about (and disdain for) the living human body and female processes in particular; (2) concentration of medical training in a handful of conservative, male-supremacist medical schools; and (3) a shocking lack of ongoing medical research on the female body.

The medical profession has become increasingly self-protective, and is close-knit to the point of intellectual incest, which is a matter of discomfort to some physicians and scientists.* This in-bred closeness severely limits medical discussion, basic research, and medical self-policing, as well as advances in the field of so-called "women's medicine." And this medical conservatism becomes self-perpetuating, for it is usually the graduates of the elite medical schools (Harvard, Stanford, Yale) who get the research plums, who chair professional committees, and who become government health advisors.

In most medical schools, whatever information is available about the female body is taught *by* males *to* males. Even those few "liberalized" medical schools that have opened their ranks to admit larger numbers of women (but still on a token basis) show a conspicuous shortage of female instructors. But something more serious is passed on from "man to man" than strictly medical data—a feeling that women are over-emotional, more intellectually unreliable than men. Whether this is direct prejudice or the product of social conditioning cannot be proven statistically, but it is a fact that men, particularly professional men, have a thinly disguised contempt for the "emotional" woman. The fact that many women do suffer eventually from psychosomatic disorders, and that such disorders are "legitimate" in the sense that pains and symptoms are *real*, is not comprehended by many members of the medical profession. Therefore, the general physician makes little attempt to cope with these illnesses.

---

* As one medical researcher (a Harvard graduate) told me with some embarrassment. "The public is unaware how many of us study under the doctor who wrote the textbook."

RESEARCH AND THE FEMALE BODY

Women are seldom used as subjects for medical research. This startling information was confirmed not too long ago at the 1974 meeting of the esteemed American Society for Experimental Biology, the largest medical research conclave in the world. I learned that fewer than ten research projects used women as subjects—in the more than 3,000 medical studies reported at this meeting. This exclusion of women from even the most basic biological research raises some serious doubts about modern medicine's knowledge of the female body.

It also has serious implications for adult women as patients. The reactions of a mature woman to a specific viral infection, humidity test, or insomnia study might vary significantly from the reactions of a college boy (the subjects used most widely in today's medical research). Nevertheless, this obvious fact seems to elude even experienced researchers, despite their interest in getting a "balanced study." (One biologist explained to me that women could be so emotional, they might "throw off the findings"!)

Surgeons have been criticized for engaging in a professional eagerness that is best described as, "when in doubt, cut it out." In self-reinforcing league with gynecologists, they have perpetrated untallied medical injustices on women. The American College of Surgeons has admitted that the majority of unnecessary operations today are performed on women. An estimated 250,000 hysterectomies take place annually in the United States. Only 20 percent of these are linked to cancer, according to biopsy reports. Many women survive this operation with enough stamina to master the emotional depressions that follow the loss of part of their sexual self; but thousands of others do not. Statistics on chronic drinking, dissolved marriages, despondency, and compulsive overeating bear witness to this. It should come as no surprise to learn that in a society in which a girl is conditioned to believe her child-bearing capability marks a large part of her human worth, her self-esteem is diminished when she is deprived of this "sexual" function.

Because of the prejudices of many male doctors (the ones who say, "If you tell a woman she's going to get a headache, she probably will"), today's woman consumer is not receiving good value for her medical expenditure.

Women patients outnumber men today. Yet modern medicine boasts more knowledge about cystic fibrosis or leukemia than women's *normal* run-of-life events: menstruation, childbirth, or menopause. No one would deny anyone afflicted with any disease, however rare, the right to enlightened medical care. But the *majority* of patients are entitled to research attention also, and to more informed expertise than the male-dominated health care profession has given to women to date.

Women could exercise a potent force at the medical cash register if they acted in boycott, or other mutual association. For whether one supports the women's movement or is a casual observer of it, all women must admit one fact: the outrage expressed by women's health collectives is beginning to make physicians look at the woman patient with new respect.

American humorist Dorothy Parker once described herself as "the greatest little hopeful that ever lived." So the health-conscious woman, investing untarnished confidence in (often misleading) television pharmaceutical commercials and magazine advertising, seeks relief in unlikely places. Or she stoically refuses to obtain medical help when it is warranted. Undermedicated, overdrugged, anemic, or angry, the thoughtful woman sees that today's expensive medical care is poorly serving its chief customers—women.

MORE LIFE NOW MEANS LONGER LIFE

If by genetic luck, common sense, or stubbbornness, contemporary woman lives past her sixtieth year, she is in good shape, at least in terms of available medical expertise. The medical hierarchy still maintains a professional astigmatism (limiting menopausal and post-menopausal endocrinal care to a handful of specialists), but the greater health care system has become more responsive to changing population trends. Large numbers of people are living longer, so senior citizen health care has provoked genuine interest; it has attracted the research investment of government and the private sector.

So if they have escaped stroke, cancer, arthritis, or other stress disorders, and haven't succumbed to accidental disabling (including the 30,000 cases hospitalized in America each year from toxic poisoning due to physician-prescribed pharmaceuticals), women can breathe easier by retirement time. Indeed, healthy women of mature years show that it is the vigorous, physically fit person who seems to live longer and better. A few chronic invalids may eke out a feeble, halfway existence, but it is usually the dedicated walker or habitual cyclist who is likely to push her life span past the ninety-year mark. "Getting the juices flowing" in itself fosters longevity.

In addition to the close link between physical well-being and longevity, surveys on Americans who lived past the ninety-five year mark revealed three striking traits in common: each one preferred simple, easy-to-digest foods; most were deeply religious; and each tried to find something to laugh about, every day. (The latter two traits help to relieve stress buildup, as we shall see in the following chapter.)

Due to recent advances in research on aging, there is greater likelihood for more people to live longer and better. Recent studies have shown how to improve the quality of body use to the point where it improves our *minds* as well as our physical selves. Although women have traditionally been victimized by medical chauvinism, the research we're going to explore in the following chapters shows that *now* women can triumph over the limitations of organized medicine. Women today have opportunities to attain a joyful new Bodypower that once was beyond their wildest dreams. This is within the grasp of every one of us.

To get the most benefit from the power-releasing techniques in the chapters that follow, it is best to begin with an inner growth experiment. Here is a self-realization exercise from the new wave of humanistic psychology.

Imagine that there are three beautiful things in the universe, each of equal beauty and each ready to be appreciated, honored, and loved. One of these is a *flower*. Another is the *moon*, as seen from earth. As you read the following chapters, let the dawning recognition of the third most beautiful thing come to you steadily and gently. Say it over to yourself; say it often and with confidence. For the third beautiful thing in the universe is—*y-o-u*.

The reader who would like to realize her true potential will repeat this exercise every morning.

CHAPTER 2
Stress and the Woman

Women have always worked, but today nearly half the women in America are working outside the home as well. At last, a paycheck rewards woman's labors—or, at least, a fraction of them—and she enjoys new independence and self-esteem. But such genetically unprecedented work directions have placed unprecedented strains upon the female body. This has resulted in a whole new set of female stress disorders: hypertension, alcoholism, strokes, smoking-induced cancers and cardiovascular disease, gastrointestinal upsets, peptic ulcers, and ulcerative colitis, just to name a few. More stress-related ills are being diagnosed almost daily.

Surveys show nearly sixty percent of all working women are married. Despite recent feminist advances, working wives get little help in coping with their fatigue and special tensions. Many unliberated husbands—perhaps acting out of a primitive sense of self-preservation—continue to insist that the working wife run the household. Medical and psychological professionals are not educated to treat this new breed of woman. When I asked for medical suggestions to help the contemporary woman handle her work-related stresses, one of the world's experts on biological stress told me there was no significant research on women and stress, *because there was no need for it*. Women, he insisted, do not have the same job motivations as men do, so scientists do not consider it worthwhile to spend time and money on such research.*

With little help outside her own resources, today's woman has chiseled out her very own stress complex of tension, guilt (especially for the working mother), and an end-of-day fatigue that leaves her body desynchronized from her mind. Her emotions race helter-skelter, while her physical capabilities are too depleted for self-control, let alone optimism. Some doctors attribute the increased sicknesses reported in women to executive and other job stress for which the female sex was not historically prepared.

But even if a woman stays at home by choice, stress is still part of her daily experience. The homemaker who can get her body in good working order can avoid frustration over household drudgery and inefficiency. When the body, runs smoothly, so does your life. Before reading further, be sure to try the following anti-stress exercise. It provides astonishing relief; if practiced daily, it will help you release tensions you never knew you had.

Stand with feet parallel, about ten inches apart, and your torso relaxed. Inclining your head backward, place your clenched fists near center back, just below your ribs (see photo). Arch your back, bend knees and breathe deeply. Now release any sounds, groans, or wails that come naturally to your lips. Hold this position about four seconds (more if needed), then return upright.

Practice this in private, so that no matter how noisy or macabre your released tension sounds, it will be for your ears only. The smiling warmth you enjoy afterward will overcome any reluctant inhibitions you feel at the outset.

---

* For a working mother (who singlehandedly paid for one daughter's college education and at that very time was anxiously budgeting for another child's tuition), such words were tough to swallow. With control, I suggested that when he had time to leave his research laboratories, he would discover labor statistics have changed considerably.

WHAT STRESS IS:
THE MEDICAL DEFINITION

Stress is best understood by first recognizing what it is *not*. True stress is not merely nervous tension, nor emotional upset, nor mental depression. Yet any and all of these factors when combined or prolonged can trigger the reaction called the *stress response*.

Dr. Hans Selye is considered the father of stress theory. In the 1930's, this Montreal physician was the first scientist to measure the effects of stress on animals, and then translate his findings into human studies. It was Selye who gave the name to the combination of symptoms known as the stress response. Whatever the stressor (cold, drugs, frustration, depression, fatigue, anxiety, rage, or other intense emotions), the endocrinal system reacts the same way to protect the body. When stress is prolonged, this three-part reaction results:

(1) The *adrenal glands* flood the body with "fight or flight" hormones.
(2) The *thymus, spleen,* and *lymphatic system* shrink. This can lower body resistance to disease.
(3) The *gastrointestinal system* is affected. Eventually stomach lesions will occur or ulcers form.

The first stage is that of *resistance,* or the rallying of body defenses. For instance, when the stressor is a skin wound, blood rushes substances to the area to seal it off. If it is a broken bone, protective swelling occurs. When the stress is emotional (such as anxiety about walking down a lonely street at night), the pituitary and adrenal glands put the body on "alert." Unless such endocrinal readiness is worked off, the reaction progresses to the third stage, and serious body disorders may result. This was seen during World War II in Britain, when English physicians became used to diagnosing "air raid ulcers." Although uninjured by the Nazi *blitzkrieg,* people would appear at medical centers for treatment, suffering from bleeding ulcers that had developed almost overnight. This direct relationship between stress and physical illness is an area of medical knowledge that was observed as far back as 425 B.C., when Hippocrates linked certain emotions to physical disorders.

WHEN STRESS BRINGS SICKNESS

A recent method of establishing the relationship between stress and physical illness was developed by Dr. Floyd C. Ring of the University of Nebraska College of Medicine. Dr. Ring created a personality test which was aimed at confirming (within less than 25 minutes) the physical ailments a person has had diagnosed elsewhere. Here is a key question from Dr. Ring's diagnostic test for readers interested in testing themselves:

> If you were sitting on a park bench, and a stranger walked up and suddenly kicked you in the shins, what would you do? [As in most research projects, this problem is male-oriented. But a woman can identify with the situation.]
>
> (a) We'd have a real showdown
> (b) I'd beat the hell out of him
> (c) I think I'd get mad
> (d) I might hit him
> (e) I'd want a reasonable explanation for such conduct
> (f) I'd probably end up doing nothing

An analysis of responses can be found on page 45. Dr. Ring found that persons prone to psychosomatic breakdowns fall into three categories: (1) those who suppress their feelings, thus blocking natural reactions; (2) those who overreact emotionally or physically; and (3) those who are unsure about what to do, or who harbor anxieties about their actions.

The Ring study identified nearly 70 percent of those persons suffering from asthma, hypertension, and ulcerative colitis. It diagnosed 71 percent of those with heart disorders, especially coronary occlusion.

Contemporary woman is victimized by her own era's range of stresses. The result is a new fatigue, insidious in that it results in increased emotional distress as well as physical exhaustion. A normal fatigue, when accompanied by the satisfaction of a job well done, can lessen stress and promote healthy sleep; but emotional stress tenses the body so that it *cannot* rest. Energy resources are drained to the point where body breakdowns occur, often followed by apathy and deteriorating self-esteem.

STRESS ON THE JOB

In addition to their share of urban crowding and commuter hassles, working women today suffer another stress that is particularly female: *fear of failure.* In a management study of women corporate executives, two Simmons College deans, Margaret Hennig and Ann Jardin, found a surprising reason for the current shortage of top women executives. Many women workers are reluctant to compete to reach top corporation jobs. They remain "all dolled up against the wall, waiting to be chosen." Those who do get chosen become competent, even expert, on one level and then begin to "peak out." They are fearful of proceeding to the next step on the ladder of corporate hierarchy. The resulting job frustration (aggravated by knowledge of the inability to push themselves) creates discontent, boredom, and fatigue. The Hennig-Jardin study advises women who wish to succeed in the business world to adopt this threefold strategy:

> (1) *Be your womanly self.* It isn't necessary to masculinize or distort your personality to compete. Self-knowledge pays extra dividends in corporate as well as private life. A woman must come to terms with herself for growth. Only then can she open

up the strong, productive relationships with others that are essential for leaps upward, into top management positions.

(2) *Don't remain a wallflower.* Speak up and take chances. Let your superiors know you are ambitious, talented, and ready to take on new assignments.

(3) *Don't be afraid of failure.* Nobody succeeds all the time. The worker who is fearful of making waves is eventually by-passed as incapable of leadership. And if you don't try, you'll never learn your true capability.

OVER-ACHIEVER STRESS

This is the opposite of fear-of-failure stress. This woman works too hard and tries her utmost, working long hours and under rigid self-discipline. Any dedicated woman is susceptible to this set of self-destructive stresses, and hard-working black women especially so. Often the first of her family to have achieved a position of prominence and good salary, the black woman can take her job so seriously she endangers her health. Black women are unusually vulnerable to hypertension and diabetes. This may be as attributable to the social stresses they face as it is to heredity.

LACK-OF-APPRECIATION STRESS

This stems from male chauvinism and corporate management clumsiness. Some male bosses find it difficult to dole out to women workers the same cordial appreciation for a job well done that they convey to men. This can bring a woman increased anxieties; she worries that she is not doing well or accomplishing enough. Over a period of time, chronic anxiety can result in serious illness.

Even when her boss makes a note to pat her on the back

(like a faithful spaniel), the gesture is seldom accompanied by long-range job advancement. Management will shrug, "Well, she got a raise. What more can she want?" What she can want, and should rightly receive, is acknowledgment and suitable promotion. Supervisors are not this restrained when it comes to distributing criticism. When something goes awry, the woman employee receives her equal share of blame.

Blue-collar workers also suffer from a lack of appreciation. According to stress studies at the University of Michigan, the lower the job status, the more likely it is that the worker will develop peptic ulcers. This partly explains the lowered self-esteem—and increasing ulcer disorders—among woman workers. Combinations of emotional and gastrointestinal distress can leave a woman discouraged, depleted, and awash with the feeling that she is unable to cope with anything.

TIME-CHANGE STRESS

Varying work schedules are a new stress factor, affecting female shift workers, telephone operators, and airline stewardesses. Studies show a minimum of three weeks is required for a worker's biological time to adapt to the stress of changing work hours. Big corporations remain stubbornly obtuse to this stress factor. One leading telephone company executive explained the unpredictable job shifts as "making the lives of our workers more interesting for them." This endocrinal upheaval, however, actually results in on-the-job ulcers and premature hearing loss for most over-30 telephone operators. (Early hearing loss is often a symptom of emotional stress.) Such disruption of one's "body clocks" brings desynchronized fatigue, indecision, anxiety, and even disturbs glandular secretions.

BODYPOWER TECHNIQUES TO MINIMIZE JOB STRESS

(1) *Find things to laugh at periodically.* Humor is an excellent way to relieve stress. Yet humor expert James C. Jones of Harvard University says that men laugh more than women. Author Erica Jong says, "I have to laugh three times a day or I get sick."

(2) *Complete a daily checklist.* At home or on the job, such a project record imbues one with a sense of accomplishment at the day's end. Also helpful: complete one specific task just before quitting time. This phases out certain endocrinal hormone discharges, helping you unwind in body and spirit. It also discourages insomnia.

(3) *Dishwash to pop rock radio.* Such bouncy, hip-moving rhythm can distract you from the tedium of housecleaning, whatever your age. And use music throughout your day. It can relieve stress. Music also works well as background for an exercise break, to replace that hostility-building coffee break.

(4) *Be your own individual.* Many mental illnesses result from trying to live your life by someone else's standards. As a noted stress expert suggests, learn to fulfill yourself according to your own lights.

(5) *Vary your routines.* Within organized boundaries, try to work more spontaneity into your day-to-day existence. Boredom gives birth to its own stress; offset this by learning the fun of experimenting. Try a new restaurant; avoid taking the same train, or driving the same road, week after week. Find your own ways to add fresh touches to the commonplace.

(6) *Return to cash.* The late Senator Robert Kennedy warned that today's computerized world was becoming stressfully impersonal: he was instrumental in having train announcers at Grand Central Station placed in glass booths, so the public could see those who spoke on the public address system. For the same reason, today's woman will find that occasionally dealing in cash is more psychically satisfying than endless rounds of checks and paper. When the currency you handle results from your own labors, this increases your self-esteem.

(7) *Discard resentments* as unworthy of you. As one social critic observed, the size of a person can be measured by the size of the thing that makes her angry.

(8) *Persuade yourself* that you're doing your utmost. Often this sidesteps overwork and hypertension. When you say to yourself, "This is the best I can do," it becomes a waste of time to worry at trifles.

(9) *Don't overload your memory cores.* Psychological stress can result from trying to memorize too much too quickly. The best bet is to take notes; then file away what you'll need. Feel free, then, to forget what is unimportant, saving your mental energies for coping with the unexpected.

(10) *Question your tenacities.* In today's world, flexibility is all-important. Many persons age themselves into a hassle by clinging to attitudes and practices that no longer satisfy or really work. Try to think about what *you* want, and then take a hard look at your lifestyle. Plan ways to get what you don't have, or learn to live better with what you have now.

LIFE-EVENT STRESS

At the 1975 meeting of the American Association for the Advancement of Science, some of the most exciting medical findings that were reported involved so-called "life events" research. A new direction in stress studies, this research shows that the number of emotional jolts or changes a person experiences within a given period of time can predispose her or him to serious disease, and even death. These changes need not be unhappy ones: a job promotion requires emotional adjustment just as losing a job requires adaptation; an upcoming wedding can be stressful as well as divorce.

Worry about loved ones can also affect female health. (For example, mothers of chronically ill children have more health problems than other women of similar age and status.) At the same time, it helps to have loved ones or friends nearby when emotional shocks occur. They will cushion stress adaptation, and prove of extra help* in this time of mobility and family disintegration.

One leading scientist has drawn up a 45-item checklist to tabulate stress influences. On a scale of 100, death of a spouse is 100, divorce is 50, marriage is 50. Change of job or the marriage of one's daughter also demand stressful adaptations, and receive high scores. Persons whose scores exceed 300 show a high incidence of disease, especially sudden cardiac arrest. Cancer, heart attacks, and disturbed behavior patterns, such as alcoholism, can also be related to stressful changes. One Chicago study on urban renewal showed that the city residents in those areas undergoing radical rebuilding had the highest incidence of psychological disturbances.

There is a factor known as social congruence (or incongruence), which is an important stress category in itself. Most communities, for instance, give social approval to women who are wives, adults and mothers, and withhold approval from women who are unmarried, adolescent and mothers. A feeling of a lack of approval subjects the individual to unconscious stress. Just how much stress depends on the individual, but without acceptance from one's peers, minds and bodies both are affected. One woman may commit suicide, another may suffer from diarrhea. One woman may become an alcoholic, another may suddenly become accident-prone.

ACCIDENT-PRONE WOMEN AND STRESS

Can stress really provoke accidents? Yes, prolonged stress predisposes a woman to suffer from one accident after another.

---

* Medical studies on laboratory animals show the presence of another of the same species seems to lessen the individual animal's stress upheaval. This illustrates a health fact key to women living alone: church work or club activity is helpful for physical well-being. Says Dr. Elmer Sterling, of Columbia University, "those who live alone, without meaningful organization participation, show a heightened disease vulnerability."

There is even an accident-prone personality. Charming and usually extroverted, such individuals are the opposite of what one would expect. They are cheerful, they like other people, and are well-liked in return. Intelligent and impulsive, they are casual about things other people consider serious and sacred—marriage, for instance. Although such people are often quite healthy (they have fewer colds than most), the accident-prone woman generally suffers from unnecessary tension. This often has an aging effect. (When the face is taut, facial lines deepen.)

Many accident-prone personalities harbor a hidden resentment of authority, traceable to a disciplinarian parent or a strict religious upbringing. Experts have found certain similarities in the emotional profiles of the accident-prone and criminals. Emotional stress seems to push one group into breaking the law, the other into breaking their bones.

Closely related to the accident-prone personality is the woman who suffers from "hurry sickness." Sometimes referred to as the "Type A personality," this concept was developed by two San Francisco cardiologists, Dr. Meyer Friedman and Dr. Ray H. Rosenman. Although at one time it was primarily men who suffered coronaries as a result of "hurry sickness," today women are joining those ranks. Of the one American in five who now dies of stroke or heart attack prior to age 60, more than 90 percent are suffering from "hurry sickness." The following questionnaire is a guideline as to whether or not you may be suffering from this syndrome. If you answer "yes," to *any* of these questions, you may be a "Type A personality."

(1) Do you feel compelled to combine daily activities, such as making shopping lists at mealtime, telephoning while watching television, or making notes as you drive?

(2) Do you habitually make certain nervous gestures, or exhibit tics or twitches? This suggests the presence of a constant inner struggle, a core part of this hyperstressful behavior.

(3) Do you tend to complete other people's sentences, feeling impatience for the slow, halting speaker? Do you secretly pity those who are not as quick-minded as you appear?

(4) Do you try to schedule more in less time? Do you make

little or no allowance for the unexpected, or for periodic rests?

(5) Do you feel vaguely guilty when you take time off and just "do nothing" for several hours or days?

(6) Do you overlook the beauty anyone can encounter in day-to-day living: department store displays, original art in an office, a flower arrangement in a friend's home, the first spring leaves?

(7) Do you regularly engage in polyphasic thought (thinking about something irrelevant) while listening to another's conversation? Do you find it difficult to refrain from bringing most conversations around to yourself and your own interests?

(8) Do you fume and overreact at traffic delays or public queues or waiting in general?

(9) Finally, are you convinced that whatever success you have had is due to your ability to do things faster than others?

STRESS AND YOUR ACHING BACK

The world's first clinic devoted to the study of chronic backache was set up by two distinguished women physicians, Dr. Sonja Weber and Dr. Barbara Stimson, in conjunction with Dr. Hans Kraus, in New York City in the 1940's. The team studied hundreds of chronic backache cases, and they discovered that more than 80 percent of all backaches that occur regularly are the result of hyperstress and lack of exercise.

The typical backache victim today is the upper- or middle-class person who gets little exercise, especially that woman whose body and nerves are regularly tensed. When muscles remain flexed they contribute to reduced body tone and unexplained fatigue. In severe cases there can be chronic tightness of key muscular groups; soon some muscles "freeze" into a contraction that persists even during sleep. With executives and desk-bound women, the tension settles into the lower neck or mid-shoulders. In women motorists, it is the lower back (or rear thighs) that bear the brunt of the unreleased tension.

Then one day, an unexpected jolt starts a muscular spasm. Without quick and specialized medical care, that spasm can turn into chronic backache. This spells lifelong agony and lifelong fatigue.

BODYPOWER TECHNIQUE FOR MINOR BACKACHES

Developed by Dr. Alexander Lowen, Bioenergetics pioneer, this exercise helps to offset back fatigue before it becomes chronic backache.

Stand relaxed, feet flat on floor (shoeless, if convenient). Bend your knees slightly, then bend from the waist and hang in a relaxed fashion. Torso drooping toward the floor, bounce gently for four seconds. Do not strain. Then touch your fingers lightly to the floor. Keep the buttocks high and your chin on your neck. Hold this "grounding" position for ten seconds, breathing normally. Practice at midday and in early evening on days you feel under stress.

STRESS AND YOUR ACHING HEAD

Everyone has a different part of his or her body that is "weak," which means that it is the first to react to stress. For many women, the neck is most vulnerable. Headache pain can be overwhelming, and not always predictable. With some women, especially cigarette smokers, headache flares just after (or in anticipation of) a stress situation. In predisposed persons, these headaches can escalate into migraines that bring almost unbearable pain. The sequence of agony brought about by a tense vascular system creating headache pain, which then creates even tenser muscles, is why some doctors give tranquilizers along with aspirin to a headache patient.

BODYPOWER TECHNIQUES
FOR TENSION HEADACHE

With increased body awareness, the woman who makes her body her best friend can recognize the early signs of headache: a tightening of the vasomotor nerves along the hairline, or a taut feeling at the back of the neck from a narrowing of the arteries supplying the cranial area. Before gulping an aspirin, which sedates headache pain rather than relieving the tension that caused it, try the following:

(1) Breathe deeply, preferably before an open window.

(2) Seated or standing, drop chin to chest (to increase blood supply to head). Hold briefly, then return upright.

(3) Using the fingertips of both hands, gently massage the back of your neck in the center. Then make four firm kneading movements; release, pause, then make four deep massage movements. Repeat four times, or until head pressure seems relieved. For vasomotor tightness, duplicate this massage sequence at your temples, just in front of your ears. Vasomotor headaches are doubly hazardous, as they restrict blood flow into the hair root area; this can lead to partial balding.

When aspirin must be taken, observe these precautions:

(1) Drink a full glass of tepid water with each aspirin dose.

(2) Breathe deeply afterward. This expedites circulation of aspirin grains from stomach to blood stream.

(3) Avoid taking aspirin in the last trimester of pregnancy.

(4) Never, never take aspirin, or aspirin-based headache remedies, if yours is a "morning after" headache. If there is any likelihood you have alcohol in your body, aspirin can cause gastrointestinal bleeding. Known to physicians as *occult bleeding*, this secret blood-letting can make you anemic.

STRESS AND ARTHRITIS

Many a woman who has had aches diagnosed as arthritis learns too late of the link between emotional stress and arthritis. This is an extra hazard for widows during bereavement. Any prolonged despondency can bring the onset of chronic diseases, such as arthritis or cancer. One pioneering health survey of widows in Australia discovered that over one-third of the women suffered alarming health deteriorations in the first year of bereavement. In the United States, parallel medical surveys show that mature women between 55 and 64 years, a time of unfamiliar and unprecedented adjustments, are most likely to suffer nervous breakdowns. Thirteen percent of all emotional breakdowns occur in such women, compared with just five percent for men of the same age. (Men during this period usually enjoy the satisfaction of peak job earnings.)

In his report on "Mourning and Melancholia," Freud took an unexpected viewpoint. He differentiated, first, between mourning (which comes with bereavement) and melancholia, or depression. Healthy mourning is psychologically useful, he suggested; it facilitates the psychic transition required in the presence of loss. In normal mourning, the bereaved weeps, yet ego strength is not destroyed. But in melancholia, or chronic depression, guilt feelings and self-accusation are often present; these inner conflicts deplete ego and energy.

In such circumstances, the body is prone to many disorders, particularly arthritis. The United States Arthritis Foundation has warned that emotional stress can trigger arthritis attacks.

There are many quack "cures" for arthritis today; even arthritis nutrition is controversial. Much can be considered extremist in the light of the great advances in drug therapy for arthritics. Many of these pharmaceuticals (such as the new family of Ibprofen drugs) have been shown to offer fewer and less severe side effects than ordinary aspirin.

Whatever the treatment, arthritis remains a disease of adaptation. It is a crippler that might be avoided by the woman wise enough to master her response to life's day-to-day stresses.

Rockefeller University's pioneer in brain studies and stress behavior, Dr. Neal Miller, notes that upset is avoided by the person who is taught in advance what to expect from a potential stress situation. Combat experiments with the U.S. Air Force showed that fear can be relieved by preconditioning. It is also important to feel one is able to do something about a problem. In shock avoidance experiments, mice taught to turn a wheel to avoid unpleasantness developed fewer stomach lesions than those who felt incapable of altering their difficulty. Dr. Miller has proposed a fascinating stress theory: fear and stress combine to increase the brain chemical called norepinephrine, and this has a euphoric effect. So it might be said that regular and periodic stress (when it motivates positive action) brings a unique kind of happiness. When a person has no environmental stress, he might not experience the self-love that results from overcoming adversity.

But the most important result in the new life events research is the recognition given to the way an individual appraises an event. It is, finally, *attitude* that determines whether a body finds fun and growth in adapting to change, or exhausts itself in joyless self-survival.

STRESS-RESPONSE ANALYSIS

Persons who responded to the quiz on page 33 by checking (a) or (b) were considered *excessive reactors* by Dr. Ring. With a personality that tends to be explosive (or seethes with desire to be so), there is a greater vulnerability to peptic ulcers, cardiovascular disorders, and arthritis.

Those who checked (f) tend to hold back their natural reactions, and are called *deficient reactors*. Many sufferers of ulcerative colitis, neurodermatitis, and rheumatoid arthritis fall into this category.

Those who are aware of their angers but who are indecisive and afraid to express their feelings would have checked (c) and (d). They are called *restrained reactors*. Such people are most susceptible to migraines, hyperthyroidism, diabetes, hypertension, and asthma.

The (e) response is analyzed as *normal* or *restrained*, depending upon the intensity or assurance of the respondent.

CHAPTER 3

How to Make Stress Work for You—Instead of Against You

Stress experts are quick to note that all stress is not unpleasant: many types of stress enrich our lives. Falling in love is stressful—but it brings psychic growth and new satisfactions. A really good party might be stressful; an exciting football game usually is. Or remember the celebration that followed your last job promotion? Or your husband's? It probably tired you, but it was a rewarding experience and you wouldn't have missed out on it. (Next time, don't be surprised if a depression or brief apathy follows any elation or exuberance. Endocrinal balance must always be restored. This is what is known as the *vis medicatrix naturae,* or the healing force of nature. As one stress doctor reminds us: What goes "up" must come "down.")

On the road to self-healing and enlightenment, it is possible to use minor stressors to revitalize oneself. Unknown to you, your body did this the last time you had a fever; the fever was a type of stressor which provoked its own cure. This stress concept is behind certain medical treatments, such as shock treatment. But you do not need to be a doctor to experiment with mild stress therapies for yourself.

There is no anti-stress formula that works for every female, for women differ in body type and emotional burdens. But if you learn how to make use of known stressors, then you can devise your own ways to get the best performance out of your body.

Cold is a stressor. Athletes, sometimes unknowingly, use the stress theory when they restore themselves with a cold shower after playing a tense game. Another stressor which is useful is physical exercise. At some Japanese factories, midmorning exercise breaks are directed by physical fitness experts, hired by management. Studies show that this practice has substantially offset stress buildup and stepped up production.

Of course many of us are not in the position of being able to take advantage of "exercise breaks." However, until American companies catch up, here are some simple exercises that can be done almost anywhere.

Any woman will benefit from twenty quick knee-bends in the ladies' room or rest area. Climbing stairs is another way to derail stress; it exercises your heart also. (Don't begin any vigorous exercise, of course, especially if you are overweight, without having a medical checkup.) But you'll also find that making a habit of using the stairs (instead of taking the elevator with all those less imaginative people) will boost both your health and your complexion. A stress-relief that is one of my favorites, and of special interest to city-dwellers, is this: jogging across the intersection at traffic thoroughfares. It is not as conspicuous as it sounds, and it's not only a healthy habit but, in big cities, an expeditious one (especially when the lights are changing). Such ready exercise is patterned after the *wind-sprint*. This is the quick energy-builder used by professional ball players prior to entering a game after a tense, inactive period of bench-warming.

Another technique applies stress to a specific part of the body, and this distracts from overall stress, or local stress elsewhere. The next time your feet are tired and aching, play a rousing record on your phonograph—and play it loudly. The noise can actually offset foot fatigue.

Many women find their feelings more painful and disruptive than the aches and pains of their bodies. But emotional stress can be diverted and helped by a few techniques. The next time you find you just can't "cope" another minute, try this: excuse your-self so you can be alone, and put on a soft, silky nightgown. Lie down, place a warm soothing cloth on your forehead. Then let your sexual thoughts wander. If your thoughts are sexual fantasies, enjoy and indulge them. After twenty minutes of "day-dreaming" like this, you'll feel more tranquil.

Of course, the need to rest quietly cannot always be met. If your good nature is really strained, and there's no way out but to hang in there, try chewing gum. As a unique form of oral exercise it works wonders to offset emotional stress, particularly when you feel rage or resentment.

Many people find travel to be an effective form of relieving stress. Although you can't run away from problems, sometimes a change of scene is the best prescription. There is no such thing as a "carefree" vacation when you're hassling with schedules, airline delays, baggage losses, foreign currency, and hotel reservations, which are all part of modern-day travel. But the distraction of unfamiliar stressors seems to provide the kind of "mind change" many people need. And, of course, travel brings promises with it: new people, new ideas, and new experiences.

The best way to travel is to go with patience as well as eager expectancy. Don't expect everything to be efficient, especially when traveling in foreign countries. If you stay calm during unexpected delay, you can enjoy your travels more, and find new experiences to be enlightening rather than stressful.

If traveling is too expensive to consider, there are similar challenges in developing an exciting hobby. Ceramics, crewel work, carpentry, boating, bridge playing, and other hobbies all use stress to distract from a stressful life.

HOW TO APPRAISE
YOUR OWN STRESSORS

In a way, understanding and making the most of yourself is the secret of Bodypower. A shortcut to this is the self-knowledge feedback that comes from taking a regular inventory of your personal stress load.

On any given day, which of the following stressors apply to you? (Check those closest to your situation.)

_____ *You smoke* more than two cigarettes in a 24-hour period.

_____ *You are anxious* that you haven't heard from your teen-aged son, wandering around Europe on holiday.

_____ *You quarreled* with your husband, or lover (or both!).

_____ *You are bored* with your job or your present lifestyle.

_____ *You are anxious* about your work, or a personal project.

_____ *You live in a high-crime residential area.*

_____ *You are overweight,* and self-conscious about it.

_____ *You drink more than a single cup of coffee* at a sitting.

_____ *You are worried* about debts, or your husband's job future.

_____ *You have impulsively made a major purchase* (new car, new fur coat) and your conscience bothers you.

_____ *You feel cold symptoms,* or a headache.

_____ *You are taking medication* (even aspirin) for the above.

_____ As a working mother, *you feel vaguely anxious* about child care arrangements you have made.

_____ *You feel guilty* you are not doing enough with your family.

_____ *You drink* more than one ounce daily of liquor, eighty proof or over.

_____ *You are emotionally involved* with the problems of a parent, or a close friend.

_____ *You are taking oral contraceptives* or feel tense and nervous because of your menstrual period (or the lateness of one).

_____ *You are taking hormones,* or other regular drugs.

_____ *You are dieting.*

_____ *Your head has been covered with a wig* more than three hours.

_____ *You have worn a figure-molding girdle* over four hours.

_____ *You would describe yourself as a nervous person.*

_____ *You have a new job.*

_____ *You have new responsibilities* in the same job. (If you have not received a recent salary increase, count this as a double stressor.)

_____ *You have moved* to a new neighborhood.

_____ *It is winter,* and you are frequently exposed to cold winds.

_____ *Your neighbors are noisy,* or your children or pet seem boisterous today.

_____ *You are depressed* for some reason.

_____ *You feel frustrated* or upset about a situation that, deep down, you know you can change but little.

_____ *You feel tired* and physically exhausted.

_____ *You have a toothache,* or are having ongoing dental repair work.

_____ *You suffer* from arthritis, backache, or other chronic ailment. (This is a double stressor if your pain is severe, or if it recurs frequently.)

_____ *You are over sixty* years of age.

_____ *You sometimes feel quite lonely,* whatever your years.

_____ *You have not been inside a church or synagogue* for over a year.

_____ *You have not spoken* to a good friend or loved one for 48 hours.

_____ *You have been in poor health* recently.

_____ *You emigrated* to this country after the age of ten.

_____ *You work or live among people who require you to speak in a language other than your native tongue.*

_____ *You have a rash,* sunburn, or other skin affliction that is itchy.

_____ *You have hypertension,* diagnosed or suspected.

_____ *You have other stressors.* (Try to identify and list. Count each separately if it has become a physical or emotional burden. These might include: A lawsuit, an unfaithful husband, a job crisis, and so on.)

SCORE ONE POINT FOR EACH LINE CHECKED

0–4. Consider this excellent if you are under 35. If you are older, and your stressors are in excess of 3, be on guard against signs of unexplained hostility and fatigue.

5–8. You have entered the stress hazard zone; proceed cautiously. You may find you are prone to respiratory infections, especially if you live in a polluted urban area.

9 or more. You may be headed for a body breakdown, if it hasn't occurred already. Rest often, and make plans to change your lifestyle. If you don't heed these warnings, be prepared for a serious illness or emotional disturbance.

If your stress score is 4 or over, try to stay away from conflict situations until your stress load is lighter. You will be prone to overreact when provoked. Also, watch your diet: stress triggers stomach upset, including indigestion or diarrhea. You will enjoy lowering your stress score through the following activities:

A ten-minute exercise session when you feel angry or intense.
OR
A distracting (even a violent!) movie.
OR
A refreshing swim, preferably in cool water.
OR
An absorbing book, especially one about a different lifestyle than your own.
OR
Detailed planning for your next vacation.
OR
A cold splash of running water on your wrists.
OR
Quiet meditation (this should be practiced regularly to be effective).
OR
Planning a new future, or a lifestyle more to your liking.
OR
Falling in love again—or readying yourself for this exciting prospect.

CHAPTER 4

The Cigarette, Alcohol, and You: Injurious to Your Health, Your Beauty, and Your Sexual Pleasure

Every day more and more women reach automatically for a cigarette when under stress. Yet, for women, the cigarette proves a fragile and shaky prop. The more nervous some women become, the more they smoke; the more they smoke, the more nervous they become. Detailed medical studies at St. Louis University have shown that smoking *will* make you nervous. These studies revealed that smoking a single cigarette disturbs hand-arm muscle mechanisms. In predisposed persons, a tremor begins that can continue for as long as thirty minutes after smoking is halted. This explains why many women who continue heavy smoking after the age of 40 develop nervous twitches.

As a former three-pack-a-day smoker, I know how smokers delude themselves into thinking that they get an electric energy charge after a quick puff on a cigarette. What they receive, actually, is the hot flare of nicotine; this triggers a speeded-up heart rate. These unnatural heart accelerations begin to affect rest time between heartbeats, and this depresses heart health.

But it is the fragile capillaries and tiny blood vessels of a woman's circulatory system that are most vulnerable to injuries from smoking. This is why women smokers experience chilly feet and hands, usually an early sign of aging and body deterioration. Smoking also encourages varicose veins, which spoil a woman's appearance. Years of smoking bring a conspicuously veiny look to the backs of the smoker's hands, making her appear years older, regardless of how trim her figure or how beautiful her face.

For women of any age, smoking interferes with sexual gratification. The vascular damage from inhaled smoke complicates and often prevents orgasm. Both men and women rely on the tiny network of capillaries that supplies the genital area to bring them to climax. In the confirmed smoker, these passages begin to degenerate early.

In today's hectic and speeded-up world, more than thirty percent of American women have become heavy and habitual smokers. It almost seems that the more liberated a woman becomes, the more she banners that hard-won freedom with the once-masculine tobacco habit.

The most alarming increase in women smokers today is among teen-aged girls, impressionable and responsive to any clever propaganda. Most of this teen-age smoking is due to the hard-edged arrogance with which the U.S. advertising industry has coolly seduced today's lucrative youth market. One company has even persuaded women athletes (most of whom are otherwise quite level-headed) to prostitute their images as symbols of physical fitness just for the sake of a winner's purse. Equally ominous for the would-be achiever is that this company has carved out for itself a product image that appeals to the liberated young woman (and often the liberated young black woman). These are the persons who can offer the most to their society, yet they are now susceptible to death-dealing hypertension (see following chapter) and cancer as a direct result of smoking.

There is no doubt that smoking shortens the life span also. The most serious effects show up shortly after the fortieth birthday. From then until age 70, smokers are hospitalized twice as often as nonsmokers.* At any age, minor sickness increases.

---

* There are few health statistics on smokers after age 70, especially for those overweight. This is not due to neglect on the part of statistics gatherers, but because of an actuarial horror: the overweight smoker is usually dead before she leaves her sixties.

Smokers have more colds, for instance, than nonsmokers. They are also very susceptible to other respiratory ailments.

A five-year study conducted in New York by Dr. Victoria A. Bradess, Dr. Henry Siegel, and Dr. David M. Spain offers unassailable evidence that women's smoking is linked to premature deaths from stroke. The researchers chose one of America's most affluent areas, New York's Westchester County, for their study. Despite high income levels, medical researchers found that those women smoking a pack or more cigarettes daily *died an average of 19 years younger* than nonsmokers.

The Westchester study found that the gap is narrowing between male and female deaths from coronary causes as well. During the fifties, there were twelve male coronary deaths for every female death. During the period of the Westchester survey (from 1967 to 1972), it was found that this ratio had narrowed to four to one.

Smoking during pregnancy is another new direction for medical research. Studies reveal the choking effect that inhaled smoke has on the developing fetus. Also, babies born to cigarette smokers are more likely to die of crib death, and they show greater incidence of respiratory problems during the first year of life. In many cases, birth weight and fetal lung development are seriously affected by the mother's smoking habits. Many women smoke because they think it controls body weight, but there is no factual basis for this belief. On the contrary, nicotine disturbs the appetite control center of the brain to the extent that one can overeat unawares. Smoking also increases the likelihood of peptic ulcers, stomach cancer, and cancer of the pancreas.* Autopsy reports show stomach ulcers are five times as frequent

---

* In these pages, we are making but passing reference to the overwhelming relationship between cancer and cigarette smoking. However, it permeates all medical thinking today. One microbiologist this author met at a social reception said he had decided to avoid all nonmedical cocktail parties for the next few years. "Knowing the statistical link between cancer and cigarettes," he explained, "I don't want to see people laughing, talking, and smoking cigarettes. It's like some bizarre Antonioni film: beautiful people partying while they destroy themselves with thin white tubes of poison."

among smokers as nonsmokers; duodenal ulcers are twice as frequent. In general, stomach tumors are forty percent more likely to kill women smokers than their nonsmoking friends.

Smoking affects a host of vital organs, but it is the oxygen displacement that affects a woman smoker's looks as well as her energies. Tiny facial capillaries supply the rich blood that creates the complexion tone; the cranial and carotid arteries convey nutrients that fortify the brain and the head, particularly affecting hair growth. Smoking constricts these vascular channels, impeding circulation, and consequently, nutrition. By the age of fifty, the woman smoker, regardless of weight, is beginning to show thinning hair and flabby skin, just like an older overweight male.

Smoking contributes not only to the deterioration of skin tissue through the loss of nutrients, but through the effect of smoke itself. Day after day, the constant presence of cigarette smoke has the same drying effect as pressing the face up against a chimney flue. Precious skin oils are dried out. The nose-to-mouth lines (called nasal-labials) are deepened, and eye crinkles begin to form. As a leading California internist concluded, after comparing the faces and smoking habits of over 1,000 patients, *smokers wrinkle earlier*.

BODYPOWER TECHNIQUES TO HELP YOU QUIT SMOKING

(1) *Purchase a small notebook,* and start a tally of each time you feel the need to light a cigarette. (In itself, this self-monitoring will help you begin to cut down on smoking.) This record will bring new knowledge about the way you have been conditioned to "need" a cigarette at certain times. Keep this record faithfully for at least four days: it will offer some surprises about yourself.

(2) *Breathing exercises* will control smoking urges. Smokers begin to depress their own oxygen intake unawares, by shallow breathing, thus further limiting their vitality. Offset this by retraining yourself. Do the following: Lie on a bed or couch with

a book placed on your abdomen. Now try to use your abdomen as a bellows—as you inhale make the book rise, then lower it as you exhale. (A yoga technique here is to empty your lungs totally as you exhale. This automatically increases your intake.) Try to establish a rhythmic breathing pattern. Then get up, continuing these movements as you stand upright. Maintain this respiratory rhythm for at least five minutes as you go about your daily tasks. (Whenever you feel the urge to smoke, practice this diaphragm breathing for four long breaths. Eventually this can discourage your smoking compulsions.)

(3) *Drastically change* your environment. Smoking urges often are prompted by conditioning cues: coffee at the table, ashtrays by the telephone. Overcome these environmental influences by redecorating, or moving those "signals" for smoking.

(4) *Remember* that, at first, you're going without a cigarette for only a few days. Then, another few days. The longer you stay away from smoking, the easier it is to remain away. Studies show if you can get through *three weeks* without smoking a cigarette, you've broken the worst of your nicotine habit.

STRESS AND ALCOHOL

Sometimes it is job stress that starts a woman drinking regularly. Or it might spring from an unhappy love affair, loneliness, or other forms of emotional stress. However it starts, consuming more than two alcoholic drinks daily can become energy-depleting.

It also starts a downward spiral that begins to erode the youthfulness of face and figure. After the age of 35, habitual drinking comes to exact a mental toll as well. Medical research at South Carolina Medical University shows that chronic drinking brings "blood sludging"—or plugged brain capillaries. When oxygen can't get through to certain brain areas, neurons die and mental efficiency declines. These side effects are a special hazard for the working woman or any person living under stress. They include wobbly memory, irrational judgment, acute nervousness, and grouchiness.

It has been said that if ethyl alcohol were to be discovered tomorrow (instead of having been handed down from Biblical history) it would be outlawed or at least restricted. For women at mid-life, chronic drinking can bring serious personality disturbances. Especially during the menopause, the aggressive action of alcohol on the psychomotor system can trigger nervous tension and, for some, insomnia. When cigarettes and liquor are combined, body vulnerability is doubled: these persons are prime cancer candidates, medical researchers report.

It is no exaggeration to say that chronic drinking can make a woman sexually promiscuous. Like certain other drugs, alcohol acts to relax social inhibitions: when drunk a person will tend to behave in ways she might not when sober. Unfortunately—as one female psychologist observed—men today are still hung up on the "good girl/bad girl" definition. Not only does the woman drinker come to lose her looks, but (as opposed to other diseases) she risks losing her husband or lover also.

Many experts now suggest that alcoholism springs from personality disturbances, many of which start in childhood. A study at Massachusetts General Hospital found that many alcoholics share certain personality traits. There is an inability to handle petty frustration: if social plans are upset, or appointments require waiting, a latent alcoholic will overreact, becoming verbally abusive or leaving in a huff. Also, many undiagnosed, or "closet," alcoholics have a misleading sociability. Affable and charming when they are sober, once they become emotionally close to someone, personal relationships tend to break down. Friendships end in hostility and unjust recriminations. Guilt follows; as expected, this leads to self-pity and more drinking.

There is a deep-rooted trait underlying all this: such drinkers have a sense of inferiority, oft-hidden under feigned superiority and boastfulness. Such alcoholics insist upon preferential treatment, repeatedly mentioning the names of celebrities or important persons. They will cite their past accomplishments and blame others for career difficulties or emotional problems.

A sense of fearfulness pervades this, for this type of alcoholic is deathly afraid of challenges. She avoids any social or job situation that would test her capabilities. One of the most curious traits found in this new breed of alcoholic is the emotional need to feel dependent upon a stronger person, including "tough" bosses or domineering friends. She denies such dependency needs amid protests of independence. Maintaining a personality balance between what is real and what is bluff becomes an emotional strain. So these "closet alcoholics" are often depressed. This brings more drinking, and negative personality traits increase with the years.

Recent studies on chronic drinkers show family background similarities. At least one, and perhaps both, of an alcoholic's parents was a heavy drinker. Genetic influences could be a factor: actress Mercedes McCambridge (an admitted ex-alcoholic) claims that medical evidence shows persons descended from Celtic and Northern European races have less tolerance for ethyl alcohol. (This might explain why there are more Irish, Swedish, English and French alcoholics than there are Italian or Jewish.) In 1973, the U.S. National Council on Alcohol Abuse reported finding a genetic defect with unusual significance. Bearers of this defect have an extra susceptibility to cirrhosis of the liver when they drink. This disorder is known as *primary type l-c*; it causes high increases of fat in the blood, and deposits of fat in the liver.

Liver health is all-important for social drinkers. In peak condition the human liver can metabolize *only one ounce* of alcohol an hour, or three-fourths of a can of beer. Drinking at a faster rate, or drinking undiluted alcohol, places an extraordinary strain on the liver, which has more than 500 tasks to perform. From beauty-building to antibody production, the aging liver should not be strained too frequently, or a diminishing hairline and mottled face will mark the results.

In the 1950's, only one out of every five alcoholics was a woman: now women are numbered as alcoholic on a *one to one* basis with men. In some areas many doctors still diagnose deaths of female alcoholics as vague nervous disorders, hepatitis, or liver infection. But the most common result of chronic and daily drinking is cirrhosis. Even in medically sophisticated New York City, in 1974 this emerged as the third leading cause of deaths (female as well as male) of persons between the ages of 25 and 65 years.

DO YOU KNOW A "CLOSET ALCOHOLIC"?

Many women today acquire a drinking problem unawares. For yourself, or a friend, the following questions will help you examine your drinking habits more objectively. (Answer "yes" or "no.")

(1) Do you have a noontime drink at least three days a week?

(2) Are you still ordering the same drink you did at 25?

(3) Is your usual drink served over ice only, or "straight"? (Martinis, bourbon-on-the-rocks, brandy, Manhattans, and so forth.)

(4) Have you come to accept the fact that New Year's Day (and other holidays) finds you nursing a hangover?

(5) Are there at least three days a week when you drink more than three drinks?

(6) Do you sometimes take a drink on weekends as a mid-morning "eye-opener" after late-night partying?

(7) Do you feel no party or celebration is really festive without liquor being served?

(8) When visiting friends, do you feel ill at ease or somehow impatient if alcoholic beverages are not offered within the first ten minutes?

(9) When faced with a disappointment, do you have the urge to "console yourself" with a drink?

(10) After work, do you look forward to "unwinding" with one or more drinks?

(11) Are you over 35 years of age?

(12) Do you pride yourself on being able to "hold your liquor"?

RATE YOURSELF

The more of our questions that you answered with a "yes," the more likely you are to have become a problem drinker. Our final question has especially serious ramifications. According to the National Council on Alcohol Abuse, the person in most danger of becoming addicted to alcohol is that person who prides herself on her drinking ability. In agreeable company, such persons imbibe more frequently, drink stronger drinks, and drink larger amounts. This brings a biochemical dependency. For the social drinker over 35, such drinking confidence is a deadly health (and beauty) hazard.

A BODYPOWER TECHNIQUE TO MINIMIZE HANGOVER

Nobody is perfect (least of all this author). There might be special occasions when you overimbibe. When this happens, do the following:

Immediately drink one or two large glasses of tepid water.

Breathe deeply before an open window for several minutes.

If possible, drink a glass of orange juice to which 2 teaspoons of brewer's yeast have been added.

The first two actions will dilute the level of alcohol in your stomach and blood stream. A vitamin boost (especially the B-complex vitamins found in brewer's yeast) will replace the vital nutrients that drinking washes from your body. This avoids the nervous tension that follows in the wake of overimbibing. It also spares an occasional drinker energy-depleting depressions and endocrinal upset.

CHAPTER 5

Hypertension: The Silent Enemy

History has a way of playing not only devilish but sometimes dangerous tricks. One of these is that certain attributes which were once considered admirable in the "genteel" woman—fainting, dizziness, and "vaporish fatigues"—are today medically recognized as symptoms of what may be killing her. At least half of America's estimated 25 million hypertensives are unaware that they suffer from this killer, precisely because of the vagueness of these symptoms. Many of these hypertensives are women. This "silent" disease, which robs women of vitality and spirit, and ages them prematurely, is usually found in persons who are overweight and over thirty. However, slim people can be candidates if they have certain personality traits.

The most ominous aspect of the hypertension specter is the difficulty of identifying the real symptoms. Busy women tend to shrug aside the early warnings of dizziness, unexplained fatigue, and headaches. By the time somebody notices the extra workload hypertension has exacted on the arteries and heart, it may be too late. When a woman is past forty, hypertension increases the possibility that she will suffer stroke or serious vascular disease.

WHEN IS HYPERTENSION REACHED?

Hypertension is diagnosed as a blood pressure reading of 160/95 and higher, a mark set by the World Health Organization. For those who live in big cities, this is a low estimate. American medical authorities prefer the definition of 140/90 as marking the topmost limit for normal blood pressure.

Of what does hypertension treatment consist? Recent medical trends call for tailoring the treatment to the patient, her individual stresses, and her lifestyle. Severe cases must be controlled by drugs. Overweight patients are told they might reduce hypertension when they trim body weight. Women hypertensives taking oral contraceptives are told to find another birth control method immediately.* Recommended in all therapies is a salt-free diet. This is followed by a medical appraisal of the ways a patient might be allowing her emotions to fan her blood pressure into a blazing health risk.

Certain personality traits predispose some women to hypertension. A revealing study at the University of California showed that hypertensives are the ones who overrespond to restlessness, anxiety, and irritability. Some can harbor hidden attitudes of resentment and defensiveness. They can overreact on casual confrontations, showing hostility; some claim to sense hostility in others, whether it exists or not.

There is another similarity in certain women hypertensives diagnosed and studied: they tend to be underachievers. Many failed to attain the social status and career growth that might be considered appropriate for their age and education. In other words, hypertensives are often underpaid and underappreciated, and they know it! (This may explain the high rate of strokes among black women, who are three times more likely to have a hypertensive stroke than white women.)

If the symptoms are so vague, you might be asking yourself, then what can you do to be sure you aren't suffering from it?

---

* After just a few months on the Pill, over 20 percent of all women show zooming blood pressure. Readings fall to normal within four weeks after the Pill is discontinued.

This is one disease where prevention also brings tranquility benefits. Below are some easy-to-follow methods to keep hypertension from taking you by terrible surprise.

DO'S AND DON'TS FOR HYPERTENSIVE PERSONALITIES

(1) *Don't* smoke. Cigarette smoking brings a rise in blood pressure with each inhaled puff. Medical studies on smoking and caffeine show that the surest way to let yourself seethe with hostility is a refreshment break consisting of two cups of coffee and cigarettes.

(2) *Do* switch to tea, or decaffeinated coffee. It is the *second* cup of coffee that most contributes to hypertension. Although tea contains caffeine, it also carries another biochemical that offsets it.

(3) *Don't* trust city tap water. Dr. Henry Schroeder, pioneer nutritionist, warns that galvanized water pipes have metal leached by the acidity of city water. Old ice cube trays plated with cadmium* offer special hazards for the hypertension-prone. They can easily be replaced with plastic trays, and bottled water used for drinking. At the very least, take the precaution of letting the water run for a few moments before drinking it.

(4) *Do* try for mood control. Many cardiologists advise patients to cultivate a "nothing bothers me" attitude. A carefree confidence works wonders to ease the lines of aging wherever they appear, inside the body as well as outside.

(5) *Do* avoid persons who hassle or annoy. Some people seem to surround themselves with magnetic fields of tension. As one

---

* Cadmium is a harsh element used for solar energy instruments. It is a cause of Japan's curious "ouch, ouch" disease. This is found around polluted water regions, and the disease name is a translation of *"itai, itai"* the Japanese expletive patients cry out when touched. Cadmium poisoning victims suffer painful joints and back. Their bones seem to break easier than other people's, due to the fact that cadmium drains calcium from the body.

Ohio country physician puts it: sometimes city people can become addicted to their own adrenaline.

(6) *Don't* let anger cripple you. Express your anger. Within sensible limits, stress experts suggest the use of anger as *strategy*. This is especially effective for the woman who is inclined to repress her disagreement, then scorch inside with discontent. Instead of letting such internal fires deform your insides, choose the occasion, then deliberately *use* anger to change things to your liking.

(7) *Do* get in touch with your feelings. This is a first step to speaking out and making a real impact on your world.

(8) *Don't* procrastinate about hypertension. Have your blood pressure checked twice a year, especially if you work or are over 35. Caught early, simple treatment suffices. When diagnosis is delayed, hypertension distorts the nerves and personality; it can interfere with your relationships with loved ones and cause a strange fatigue by day's end. Called "the silent killer," hypertension requires constant vigilance. It so depletes energy that it is said becoming "just a little bit" hypertensive is like getting "just a little bit" pregnant.

CHAPTER 6
Vitality and the Beauty Glow

Feminists say that many women place too much emphasis on outward appearances. I agree, of course, that society must learn to regard a woman for what she is, not merely for what she looks like. At the same time, when a woman knows she is looking her best, she feels her best. And regardless of her own beliefs, a woman must deal and traffic with those who might not be as enlightened as she. At any age, a well-groomed appearance counts for much. There is a German saying—*the handsome woman is always right*—which expresses this.

One unique aspect of our Bodypower regimen is that the same exercises that build energy also enhance good looks and promote a glowing, radiant complexion. This is because the basis of body energy and glowing skin are really the same—good circulation. Strenuous exertions are not essential. A few simple daily exercises, augmented by an active lifestyle, will cultivate the rosy glow that everyone wants to acquire. Improved circulation pays other beauty dividends: gleaming hair, sparkling eyes, a more graceful carriage. Less obvious but no less rewarding is the increased sexual response which comes with our Bodypower exercise sequence (see the following chapter).

For the woman who wants to be both healthy and beautiful, good circulation is absolutely essential. Circulating in the body's

75,000 miles of blood canals, blood offers two vital properties: (1) red cells, which carry hemoglobin, the oxygen-carrying element; and (2) white corpuscles, which protect the body against infection. The physically fit woman is also the sexy woman. Sex therapy counselors advise that sexual orgasm is achieved more readily by women who have good circulation. This is due to the fact that just prior to orgasm, blood rushes to the opened capillaries of the genitals, thus supplying the extra oxygen needed for the tremendous contraction of climax. (If you remember, I explained in Chapter 4 how smoking can ruin an orgasm, since nicotine has a detrimental effect on the circulatory system.)

VITAL BLOOD AND NATURAL ENERGY

Many women suffer from a major enemy of good blood: anemia. Iron deficiency anemia is the best known form, although other kinds can result from vitamin B-12 deficiencies or metabolic disorders. Anemia can be a "secret" disorder, for many anemic women seem to have no symptoms. Fatigue is the most common symptom, but it is possible to be anemic and not feel tired. Many women who are anemic unawares are those taking oral contraceptives or wearing intrauterine devices.* Blood cell counts vary widely among women, and oddly enough the fatter you are, the less likely you are to be anemic. (Extra pounds require extra capillaries—hence the cardiovascular strain from obesity.) If your doctor finds you have a red cell count below four million per cubic millimeter or above six million, it suggests an abnormality. To be sure you are not anemic you should have a blood analysis twice a year, and four times a year if you take oral

---

* So common is secret anemia in prosperous lands today due to so-called "occult bleeding" that it is likely that the reader suffers from low-blood fatigue, especially if she: (1) is underweight; (2) is of menstruating age; (3) uses one of the birth control methods mentioned above; (4) resides in a warm climate; or (5) is a vegetarian.

contraceptives or use an I.U.D. (Insist that your gynecologist do this when you go for renewal of your Pill prescription.)

HOW EXERCISE ENRICHES YOUR BLOOD SYSTEM

Exercise steps up the production of red blood cells in the body. Here's what happens: with exercise, the kidneys are notified that more oxygen is needed. They release a substance into the bloodstream, which carries it to the bone marrow; there it triggers an increase in red cell production. As more red cells join the ever-circulating bloodstream, the body's oxygen-intake and distribution capability is expanded. This relationship between fitness and blood quantity is so direct that a woman can increase her amount of blood by nearly a quart after she achieves circulatory health.

Augmenting one's blood supply aids energy in an unexpected way: it dissipates the feeling of sluggishness that is often mistaken for apathy or boredom. Once metabolic wastes are quickly removed from body parts by an alert circulatory network, a secondary fatigue is stripped away. As Southerners say, "You begin to feel perky."

When you learn to make optimal use of your body, even workaday routines become less tiring. Suddenly one day the same exertion that once seemed difficult becomes effortlessly simple—and fatigue vanishes. This is due to another body area that exercise benefits: the lungs. It should be noted that those exertions that are most rewarding are those that benefit what I will term the rejuvenation areas (the lungs and the heart). Such exertions are those that require lung power, such as running (or strenuous walking), cycling, and tennis. After just a few weeks of such exertions, the oxygen intake ability will notably improve. (Stamina, or the ability to sustain prolonged physical exertion, can be measured in terms of *the rate of oxygen consumption per unit of body weight.* Scientists now use a mathematical formula to express this relationship: VO_2 max in L/min.

While scientists have not, at this writing, measured female stamina, there is promising medical research on men. In Scandinavia, the oxygen-utilization abilities of professional lumberjacks were measured and compared to their job productivity. These men were paid on a piecework basis. It was found that those with high oxygen utilization ratings did more work and earned more money. Another study, this one among sugar cane workers in Colombia, also demonstrated that *lung development* improves work stamina.

During the middle and later decades of life, fitness becomes even more important. After the middle thirties, the body's ability to utilize oxygen begins to deteriorate.

CALISTHENICS ARE NOT FOR EVERYBODY

It is appropriate here to set right a popular misconception: calisthenics, or exercises, are not the answer for physical fitness; they are only one part of the fitness picture. No matter how chic or noted or elegant the exercise salon, if their specialty is confined to exercise and exercise equipment, such activity alone will not keep you fit. Nor can exercise reduce body weight significantly—unless it is accomplished by a calorie-reducing diet.

Indeed, the woman who is more than twenty pounds overweight should diet before she starts to push and pull her present weight. Her already burdened heart and vascular system can be strained by unaccustomed exertion. Some exercises turn fatty tissues into hard muscle, thus making excess weight difficult to remove—especially for a woman over 35. Membership in an expensive exercise salon is not the only road to fitness. Many women discover that such membership holds no magic formula, and they become early dropouts. Then "quitting" becomes a psychological defeat, as well as a physical one. In itself, this can lead to overeating and weight gain.

Another individual for whom gymnastic exertions may prove to be a serious mistake is the anxiety-prone woman. A landmark study at the Washington State School of Medicine showed that strenuous exercise may induce anxiety neurosis in some people, due to biochemical changes. Such changes cause a rise in blood lactate, a normal metabolism by-product, but one that can build to pathological levels in certain persons. An estimated ten million Americans, many of them undiagnosed and most of them women, are afflicted. For such persons, intense physical activity aggravates those anxieties that are already present, bringing insomnia, breathlessness, chest pains, feelings of apprehension, nervousness, and unexplained fatigue.

Many women sufferers notice this increased anxiety and worry about it; thus it brings self-doubts. However, medical research shows that increased anxiety due to blood lactate is a biochemical problem that can have definite physical causes. Compared to normal subjects, anxious individuals are unable to 'maintain strong handgrips. They react early to noise levels, as well as light intensity and heat. With any external discomfort their breathing rates quickly increase. If carbon dioxide is added to inhaled air (as in public gatherings and crowded rooms), they seem to breathe faster. They also sigh more. Even with light exercise, such people have higher pulse rates; they use inhaled oxygen less efficiently. Without medical supervision, exercise salon exertions can actually be harmful to these women.

Women who have long been inactive may notice an unexpected fatigue after strenuous physical exertion. This is due to a biological law known as the *oxygen debt*. This phenomenon permits exertions beyond the body's immediate capability for oxygen intake. During this time the body compensates for insufficient oxygen by slowing down on many vital processes (including the disposal of that lactic acid that has piled up from muscular contractions). Once exertions are halted, deep respiration gradually replenishes the needed oxygen stores and metabolic wastes are removed. The informed woman knows that her best bet is to wait out this period of chemical fatigue. She should breathe deeply, preferably before an open window.

There is no denying that all body parts benefit from daily usage. Yet (as the late Dr. Paul Dudley White and others showed) it is stop and start activities that are advisable for the fitness beginner: brisk walking, cycling, swimming, jogging. Also important is the fact that many women find it easier to relax emotionally on a solitary walk rather than in a hectic exercise salon. Therefore, for a variety of reasons, whether you suffer from overweight, anxiety, or just plain laziness, it will probably be more beneficial to work out your very own fitness formula than to follow blindly the routine workout in a commercial exercise salon.

EXERCISE AND BRAIN POWER

Making good use of one's body in a daily program not only slows the effects of physical aging but also improves mental efficiency. Once the body's oxygen transport is revitalized, brain cells benefit, just like the rest of the body.

This has been medically proven. Elderly patients at the Veteran's Hospital in Buffalo, New York, were given oxygen treatments for 15 days, two sessions daily, with tests taken before and after therapy. Mental capabilities—especially memory ability—improved, and scores on standard I.Q. tests jumped as much as 25 percent.

In California, physicians studied a group of senior citizens (all men) who volunteered to participate in a mental stamina-physical fitness program at the University of Southern California's Gerontology Center. Three times weekly, the group practiced simple stretching exercises, jogged, walked and swam. The physical improvements were substantial: waistlines were trimmed, body weight redistributed and blood pressure normalized. But the most surprising changes came in personality and attitudes. Every participant showed higher mental performance and a renewed ease in acquiring new skills. And, most gratifying, all reported that this fresh new agility brought a new joy in day-to-day living.

For everyone, recreational fitness is extra beneficial if you endeavor to link mind and body in communion. When exercising, concentrate on those body parts that are being moved. Israel's Dr. Moshe Feldenkrais, one of the new psychophysical scientists, recommends making jogging a spiritual meditation.

Disciplined fitness practice can help you acquire a form of enlightenment or *sadhana*, says Esalen Institute's Michael Murphy. Daily practice, rain or shine, can develop *siddhi*, the Sanskrit phrase describing the supernatural and unusual powers that mortal man is capable of achieving. Such liberating physical discipline brings new inner vision, as if the doors of perception were suddenly thrown open. A more enlightened person will emerge—you begin to understand what self-love, and universal understanding, are all about.

Now, here is a true/false quiz to test your understanding of true physical fitness:

WHAT'S YOUR FITNESS I.Q.?

Answer true or false.

(1) Jogging is not only cheaper than membership in an exercise salon—it also benefits the body more.
(2) Exercising indoors benefits the body as much as outdoor exertion.
(3) Well-designed exercise equipment can keep you fit if it is used faithfully.
(4) A brisk, 15-minute walk daily will keep you as fit as a weekly tennis game.
(5) Swimming is as good for fitness as cycling or jogging.

TRUE/FALSE TEST ANSWERS:
(1) *True.* It is a fitness fallacy to equate gym workouts with deep-breathing, or aerobic conditioning that stimulates the circulation and vital processes.
(2) *False.* Outdoor exercise brings bonus benefit, due to the intake of fresh air. Idea: when outdoor exertions are incon-

venient, why not place your exercise equipment or stationary bicycle before an open window?

(3) *False.* In addition to the reasons mentioned above, stretching and calisthenics only exercise the outer muscle belts of the body. Inner organs (especially heart and lungs) must be exerted and exercised before the fitness condition—and a glowing skin tone—are achieved.

(4) *True.*

(5) *False.* Swimming has its revitalizing benefits, particularly for those over 60, who need spinal flexibility. But it is an overrated fitness endeavor unless you are a year-round swimmer of championship capability. It is all too easy for most of us to while away time in locker room conversations, or lounging poolside, rather than swimming uninterrupted end-to-end pool laps. A minimum of 15 pool laps, twice weekly, is required before swimming can qualify as a serious fitness activity.

SCORE YOURSELF:
Count 20 points for each correct answer.

If you score 80 to 100, you're probably better-looking than most of your contemporaries. Congratulations!

If you score between 40 and 60, you're an underachiever in terms of what your body can do for you, and vice versa. (You're also missing out on lots of fun.)

If you score under 40, shape up! If quiz ignorance relates to your lack of fitness activity, this book can turn a new page in your life.

CHAPTER 7
Six Minutes to Bodypower

Tension drains energy the way vampires were once thought to drain blood. Many factors (fatigue, emotional upset, and environmental stress) can cause tension, which then affects everything else that you do. (Just recall the way too-tight shoes can tense your nerves and warp your outlook!) In a woman's body, the main areas of susceptibility are the back of the neck, the shoulders and middle back, the lower back, and the back upper leg muscles.

You can dissipate such energy-draining tensions with the Bodypower Exercise Sequence, based partly on Yoga, and partly on newer scientific theories. This six-minute exercise series can be practiced by any active woman at any time of the month. The exercises are designed to release trapped energy and relax body rigidity. Most important for the woman of 30, they can *slow the aging process*. The exercises stimulate circulation, so that you get that beauty glow after performing them as well as feeling refreshed. The sequence is important, for this careful progression of one into another brings special rejuvenation benefits.

A six-minute exercise sequence at bedtime (or just after work) helps offset tension buildup on stressful days. I do the exercises in bathing suit or leotard. You might prefer pants or shorts. The important thing is to feel unrestricted, so no girdle or confining undergarments should be worn.

Open a window and turn on some bouncy background music (this speeds muscular relaxation). Spread a sheet or bath towel on the rug (you will want to get down on the floor for certain exercises), and provide yourself with a small pillow. Try to clear your mind of anything and everything outside yourself. Focus your thoughts on each body part as you move it. Don't rush yourself. Let your motions flow gracefully from one into another.

Stand up and prepare to relax!

THE SIX-MINUTE BODYPOWER EXERCISE SEQUENCE

(1) Stand straight, body relaxed. Stretch your arms, upward, first one and then the other, as if you were climbing two ropes. Reach forward and upward, really stretching your shoulders as you move. Repeat three times with each arm.

(2) Now relax your body, and bend at the waist. Let your body hang limply as it droops toward the floor. You needn't touch the floor, just bob up and down for several seconds. At extreme position, hold head and shoulders down for a count of four. Return to upright position.

(3) Droop body again, this time tucking your head low, between your shoulders. Inhale and exhale slowly, and continue breathing for 20 seconds. Bend your knees slightly and touch fingertips to floor. Let the blood flow to your brain (and your complexion!). Now return upright and continue to breathe deeply, using your abdomen as you exhale.

(4) Lie down on your tummy, with your hands under your 'chin, fingers touching, palms down. Once in position, raise your head and shoulders, using a half-elbow lift. (See Illustration #1.) For the first three days, stop here. On the fourth day, go on to (4b).

(4b) When you feel supple, push your entire upper torso up

with your arms. Make a special effort to keep your legs loose and relaxed. Repeat twice. (See Illustration #2.)

(5) Again lie flat on your tummy on the floor, and place arms at sides. Now press your fists into the floor as you raise your legs together as high as is comfortable. Repeat twice. Do not force this: your spine becomes more flexible little by little as your body rejuvenates. (See Illustration #3.)

(6) Now sit tailor-fashion, with your legs crossed. Place your palms across your abdomen, gently but firmly. Try to soothe your body as you breathe deeply.

(7) Now bend forward, resting the tip of your forehead on the

pillow, placed just ahead of you. Hold this position and count
to six. Then return to a sitting position. After one week, try to
continue breathing while your forehead is on pillow. This is the
famous *yoga mudra*, which is supposed to arouse the dormant
energies at the base of the spine.

(8) Still sitting tailor-fashion, give two minutes to serene
meditation, prior to psychic return to your immediate environment. If meditating during daylight, place your fingers in the
position illustrated in #4. After sundown, reverse this, placing
palms up. (To increase the self-healing potential of this inter-
lude, permit this thought to run through your mind: "Let there

be no distortions of body, mind or spirit." This is a prayer originated by a noted Pennsylvania Dutch faith healer.)

(9) Sit on the floor now with legs outstretched. Raise your arms and bend gracefully backward. Hold briefly, then return upright. Then bend forward, reaching toward your toes. Try to really stretch those lower back muscles, and tuck your head low.

(10) Lightly grasp knees and arch your torso, placing your head on your knees. Hold in extreme position for a fifteen count, then return upright. At first this may seem rigorous; but this is a key yoga exercise for releasing trapped energy in the shoulders and neck. As your neck becomes more flexible, you will come to enjoy the tension release that follows. (After a few days, try to hold for a count of thirty.)

(11) "Unwind" your body with a return to the backward bend, arms lifted. Repeat twice, then return to an upright position and rest briefly.

A BODYPOWER FITNESS ALTERNATIVE

The Six-Minute Bodypower Exercise Sequence will release tensions, but it should be supplemented with a fitness activity that will exercise your lungs and heart, also. *Rope-skipping* is one of my favorites. It works wonders by stimulating circulation.

Combined with our Exercise Sequence and an active lifestyle, this fitness system will keep any normal woman fit, giving her physical coordination and self-confidence.

If you haven't been physically active in recent months, start with 60 rope turns daily. If this is tiring, rest briefly. (Be sure to breathe deeply to make up that "oxygen debt" described earlier.) Try to work up to 150 jumps within the next two weeks. Rope-skipping is more fun when you do it to a musical accompaniment; this makes early missteps less irksome, and brings a graceful rhythm to your body movements.

A BODYPOWER TECHNIQUE:
CHART YOUR FITNESS GAINS

For added interest (and new self-love), keep a progress record of your Bodypower gains. You'll need:

(1) A stopwatch (or any clock with a second hand)
(2) A lined sheet of paper (graph paper is best)
(3) A pencil

Set up a chart, with dates to be written in every day you practice this fitness activity (best done daily, but at *least* three times a week). Begin by recording your pulse rate at rest. (This can range anywhere from 70 to 100 beats a minute; later on, this will stabilize, as your cardiovascular system is exercised on a regular basis.) Then record your pulse rate after 60 rope turns.* Again, in five minutes, record pulse rate.

You will be approaching your optimal fitness condition when your pulse returns to normal *within five minutes* of 150 rope turns. Don't worry if your heart races after the first few sessions. Practice will produce stamina and boost vitality.

Over the next four to six weeks, repeat this rope-skipping exercise at least three times weekly. By the time your heart/ pulse rate shows it can quickly adapt to simple exertion, you will be noticing definite beauty improvements also. This is because you are building new blood capillaries, bringing the glow of youth to your face. Such complexion benefits will be increased if you lie down, for a few minutes, after exercising.

---

* If you are more than 20 pounds overweight, begin this (or any other) exercise gradually. Your best bet: schedule a daily 15-minute walk for two weeks prior to beginning a more strenuous exercise program.

CHAPTER 8

Sleep: Energy Builder or Beauty Destroyer?

While many people talk about getting "a good night's sleep," they often do much to discourage it. Worried that sleep won't come, they toss fitfully with body motions that excite the mind rather than soothe it, or take drugs (robbing themselves of the most energy-restorative sleep stage: *delta sleep*), or down a tranquilizer or a shot of liquor just before bedtime. What depressants such as alcohol and some drugs actually do is disrupt and shorten the regularly occurring sleep stages. This results in four A.M. awakenings and morning stupors.

Many self-termed insomniacs may be suffering a unique sleep problem, one in which the sleeper remains in the lightest sleep stage. Other insomniacs actually sleep without realizing it. They are dreaming they are awake. A new illness brought about by insufficient sleep has been identified as a kind of pseudo-arthritis, which brings body aches and a swelling in muscles and joints. In turn this makes the individual so uncomfortable that it is difficult to drift into healing sleep.

Fortunately much has been discovered recently about these "new" sleep disorders. It has also been scientifically established that the proverbial eight hours a night are not essential for everybody; individual sleep needs can vary from four to as much as ten hours.

The new "sleep science" was born on university campuses, during the early fifties, when psychologists set up sleep clinics to identify and electronically trace sleepers' brain wave patterns. As a result, since 1952, scientists have learned more about the sleep phenomenon than had been learned in all the centuries before then.

Can indigestion disturb one's dreams? Yes.

Do neurotics and sex criminals have different sleep patterns from normal persons? Yes.

Can sedatives bring restorative sleep? Not really.

Is dreaming essential for emotional health? Yes, for the vast majority of persons.

As with most other medical research, the first sleep studies involved male college students. However these campus facilities have since grown into sophisticated sleep clinics. Many are now open to private patients, a fact which has boosted the input of female sleep histories for data banks.

The normal person, scientists agree, gets to sleep and then rests in a sequence of stages. The orderly journey from Stage I (light sleep) through Stage II (deeper) then into Stages III and IV (deepest sleep, known as delta sleep) is a key to mental and physical vitality. These sleep sequences occur several times nightly (some scientists say every 90 minutes). At the end of each cycle the sleeper enjoys a REM dream. This REM sleep is particularly important for women.

REM SLEEP AND ENERGY

The first sleep scientists to measure brain waves during sleep, using an electroencephalogram, found a wonderful consistency about REM sleep: persons awakened during the REM stage always remembered dreaming. Dream-memory was less reliable during other sleep stages. An emotionally healthy person dreams several times a night, usually during the REM sleep stage. It is during REM sleep that many body changes occur. This is a time of emotional excitement, when brain temperature rises and oxygen is metabolized more quickly. In males, penile erections occur. If you suffer from duodenal ulcers, this is a hazardous period, for it is now that gastric acid is secreted in response to vivid dreams or nightmares. There is also often an increased supply of adrenaline to the bloodstream during REM sleep.

REM sleep time seems to increase when the sleeper's daytime activity involves new tasks. An ingenious experiment involving Denver medical students illustrates this. They wore goggles that distorted their vision throughout the waking day. Each night, their sleep phases were electronically measured. Early in the study the volunteers discovered that they had to take special care with such intricate tasks as shaving and writing. These first nights their brain wave tracings betrayed a supernormal amount of REM sleep. But once their eyes (and optical brains) had learned to master difficult tasks, the nightly amounts of REM sleep dropped to normal. A Boston study revealed that patients with speech difficulties had extensive REM sleep on days when they were given special speech coaching.

But REM dreams do not bring psychic equilibrium for all (as was thought in the early days of sleep studies). Chronic depressives might be better off with little or no REM sleep. The reason may be found in the *dream rebound* disorder that is seen in patients at addiction treatment centers. Those addicted to sleep-influencing drugs (including alcohol and barbiturates) can have such terrifying REM dreams that they are driven back into the arms of their habits. (New therapy forewarns the addict of this dream syndrome and gives backup counseling that increases the patient's self-assurance.)

Sleeping pill users awaken with a feeling of sluggishness, which, researchers have discovered, is due to REM sleep deprivation. Whether the sleeper's body has become tolerant of the drug or not, it remains sedated long hours after drugs are metabolized. This interrupts normal endocrinal discharges and other body rhythms. And all hypnotic drugs become useless after three to four weeks of usage. The sleeper who continues to find drugs useful has become psychologically addicted. Because she believes the sleep potion is effective, she relaxes and sleep comes naturally.

HOW WE CONDITION OURSELVES
TO SLEEPLESSNESS

A conducive sleep environment is thought to be a major factor in successful sleep. Behavioral training has done much for sleepless persons, gradually reconditioning their reactions to those bedside implements that have become cues for alertness: the bedroom lamp and table, clocks, and late night television. Sleep scientists caution against turning on a light and beginning to read in bed if you are not able to sleep. If after ten minutes, you have not fallen asleep, it is better to leave the bedroom—or at least leave your bed. Tossing and turning is counterproductive. Relaxation comes easier away from the problem environment.

Worldwide sleep research shows that many troubled sleepers need not be anxious about their sleeplessness. What is important to health is the orderly repetition of structured sleep stages; the amount of sleep time is secondary. Two bizarre cases (of an Australian and an Italian farmer) were investigated and authenticated: they are able to function normally with little or no sleep. A New England woman in her seventies was worried that she only obtained four hours' sleep nightly. Monitoring of her sleep patterns showed that she had remarkably efficient sleep: she went quickly into deep delta sleep, then "came up" and glided gently into REM dreams. ("She was sound as a bell," said her sleep consultant.)

Some of the world's greatest achievers trained themselves to get by on little sleep.* Thomas A. Edison's self-discipline was legendary—four hours of sleep at night, with brief catnaps

---

* The eyelid puffiness that is associated with lack of sleep can be the result of sinus congestion or a post-nasal drip, as fluid accumulates in the greater eye area. Suggestion: make sure your head is elevated at least six inches, especially during early morning sleep hours.

throughout the day. American dermatologist Dr. Norman Orentreich (who developed the hair plug transplant and earns in excess of $550,000 a year at his Manhattan clinic) sleeps just four hours a night. He explained to me that he taught himself to sleep this way while in the U.S. Navy, serving in World War II. Assigned a tour of duty that required four hours on watch, then four hours off, he discovered he didn't require the second four hours to function efficiently.

Proper nutrition can promote deep sleep. The sleep scientists agree on the biochemical importance of *serotonin*, a brain chemical that seems to trigger sleep onset. It also brings the profound sleep known as delta sleep. Serotonin is made in the body from tryptophane, a multi-purpose nutrient found in high-protein meats and foods like cheese and whole milk. (This is why one feels groggy after eating a large steak.)

Warm milk at bedtime can hasten sleep onset, and one reason for this is rooted deep in the psyche. (As one sleep scientist suggests, "Warm milk smells like mother.") There is nutritional justification as well, because milk is high in calcium, which can relax nerves and muscular tensions.

It is natural for women to require less sleep with advancing age. (Less nightly sleep, that is; one is reminded of Yeats' description, "When you are old and gray and full of sleep, and nodding by the fire . . .") Whatever one's age, it helps to distinguish between quick naps—even when they relieve eyestrain— and the deep sleep stages that contribute the most to energy and emotional renewal. For there are definite body rhythms that the sleeper can tap to obtain deep, restorative sleep.

WHEN A NAP REPLENISHES ENERGY (AND WHEN IT CANNOT)

Sleep Stage IV is the deep sleep that small children enjoy when they are carried home late from family gatherings, unconscious to the world. This is the sleep stage when the body has the greatest activity in HGH, the human growth hormone, giving rise to the legend that body cells regenerate most during sleep. It is early evening sleep that rewards one with ready Stage IV sleep, a contemporary medical agreement with the folk wisdom that "one hour's sleep before midnight is worth three after."

While elderly persons complain of their inability to obtain such deep sleep, often this is due to their own self-destructive daytime habits. The lonely and the eccentric can desynchronize their body rhythms by eating at odd hours. Strict food schedules have been found to improve sleep patterns, even for the testy sleeper.

Most women don't recognize the important relationship between the time of their nap and its energy-restoring potential. If you are emotionally drained, an early morning nap will give you REM dreams to stabilize your mood. A midday nap can ease eyestrain and derail stress buildup. But it is the early evening nap that will leave you bright-eyed and ready to cope (and ambitious enough to swim the Hellespont!).

Day or night, a regular sleep habit is useful. Making a ritual out of preparing for bed helps your body ready itself for the descent into drowsiness. Brushing your teeth, removing makeup, brushing your hair, and putting on a soft, nonbinding night dress —all these are sleep cues, especially when repeated in the same sequence night after night.

Good sleepers experience a temperature decline as sleep approaches and body temperature continues to fall during sleep, reaching its lowest point in the early morning. Just one hour prior to waking, temperature starts to climb, reaching normal as the sleeper starts to open her eyes. Problem sleepers show a higher rectal temperature before and during sleep. After they do get to sleep, they have higher pulse rates than easy sleepers. Some unfortunates also have sharp finger constrictions. Whether as a cause or effect, poor sleepers are more inclined to be neurotic. Such emotional turbulence reminds one of the German proverb: "*Die böse Geister schlafen nicht,*" or, "Evil spirits don't sleep."

Whatever your age, if you are troubled by chronic sleeplessness, you would benefit from expert sleep diagnosis. In some cases the sleep difficulty can be a secondary symptom, masking a disorder that has been pushed from awareness during the waking day.

A typical sleep problem is that of the sleeper who awakens frequently during the night. Such insomnia is tiring. The sleeper usually believes she is getting less sleep than indeed is the case. Persons who are unable to return to sleep, some psychologists say, may suffer from a psychogenic depression. This clears up with psychotherapy, and sleep languors are returned. Sleep counseling is imperative, however, for the disorder becomes an energy-destructive cycle: studies show that depressed persons are those most easily awakened by external stimuli, such as dripping faucets, clock tickings, and car horns.

BODYPOWER TECHNIQUES TO GET THE MOST FROM SLEEP

Begin mentally preparing for sleep shortly after finishing your evening meal. Avoid rousing debates or heated argument. Do not smoke. Don't work on business problems that entail mental agility. Decline all caffeine-bearing beverages, including colas. Avoid TV programs and books that excite rather than comfort and soothe.

THEN

Begin the bedtime rituals described previously in this chapter (brushing teeth and so forth). Leisurely stretch your body, catlike. Jiggle each arm and ankle to release entrapped tensions. And then get into a loose-fitting, pretty nightgown.

THEN

Slow down on all intense thinking, especially about emotional problems. If emotionally upset, practice our Bioenergetic anti-stress exercise (see Illustration 1 on page 76) at least four times.

THEN

Drink a glass of warm milk. My own favorite sleep-inducer is a chocolate-flavored milk drink, just barely warm. Drink slowly, cutting down on sudden physical movements as you slow down mental activity. If you are a troubled sleeper, augment this with a calcium lactate tablet, available anywhere without prescription.

THEN

Enter your bed quietly, if sleeping alone. (If not, and intercourse is in the offing, welcome it: there is no sleep as restorative to beauty as that slumber that follows sexual fulfillment.) If alone and restless, begin deep abdominal breathing. *Do not count sheep:* this sparks mental attention. Rhythmic breathing becomes a soporific through the monotony of its repetition.

THEN

Start to deliberately relax body parts, beginning with each toe, and moving very slowly up the body. Let this limpness work its way up to your head, and don't feel shy about trying to relax your ears and, most important, your jawline.

THEN

Let your thoughts wander, perhaps unfolding a fantasy, even a whimsical one. Studies show that ridiculous, lightly humorous thoughts induce serotonin discharges which speed the onset of sleep. Let your thoughts idle and image reel. Things are now different from the way they seem in daylight, perhaps better, and you are floating . . . away.

CHAPTER 9

Your Body Clocks: How to Use This New Knowledge for Better Health, Better Looks, More Energy—and Better Sex

Just as there is a rhythmic sequence to the rise and fall of ocean tides, and as eclipses of the sun occur at predictable intervals, so there are regularly occuring events within the human body. When our body rhythms are on schedule, we enjoy robust vitality. When our body "clocks" become desynchronized, we feel apathetic, indecisive, or grouchy.

Now the new science of biorhythms can equip us with the kind of self-knowledge needed to attune ourselves to emotional "ups" and "downs" at certain times and the wondrous rush of energy waves at other times.

The ability to chart body periodicities is acquired with greater ease than one might believe. (Women learn early how to calendarize that key biorhythm, the menstrual cycle.) The new biorhythm technology grew out of the recognition that industrial workers have days when they are especially accident-prone. Scientists have learned we show intellectual "highs" and "lows," as well as emotional and physical rhythms.

These result, indirectly, from the clockwork regularity with which biochemical events build and fall within the body. In the previous chapter we discussed the way body temperature drops, preparing us for sleep by bringing drowsiness. So, also, gamma globulin rises in the blood during the last six hours of the day.

And body triglyceride levels rise and fall in a sequence that peaks around 6 A.M. in most individuals. This is also the time when adrenal hormones are highest. Other changes in body chemistry occur with predictable regularity.

It is the emotional biorhythm that offers special insight for women. This shows us how the same person will react calmly to unexpected difficulty one day, yet be distraught on another. In extreme instances, these biorhythms can influence one to the point of madness. A Rhode Island psychologist, Dr. Lucien C. Sansouci, using special patient charts, can predict when inmates at his hospital are likely to cause disturbances. One patient, Charlotte D., spent 210 days in seclusion before a study of biorhythms brought medical insight into her condition. The extreme changes in this patient's cycles caused her to be lovable when her cycles were high and quite dangerous when low. She would scream, bang the wall with her head, recognize no one, and be possessed by an obsession with killing when her biorhythms were unfavorable. When favorable, her physician reported she became docile, even loving and happy. "Then she asks me to marry her," Dr. Sansouci notes. "She promises me beautiful children. . . . She sings, jumps with joy." One glance at her biorhythm chart tells him what to expect shortly.

Other inmates have been diagnosed as victims of a similar malady, loosely termed *folie circulaire*, or cycled insanity. Such a peculiar psychosis afflicted the writer Mary Lamb (sister of the English essayist Charles Lamb), who became a celebrated case in the eighteenth century. She was enormously fond of her mother, yet killed her during a temper tantrum. The courts were persuaded to place the girl in her noted brother's custody. There she led a fruitful life for another fifty years, although this period was interrupted regularly by psychotic attacks, some thirty-eight in all. At the first sign of one, her brother would rush her to a hospital. Upon recovering, Mary would resume her writing and socializing with no hint of aberration; she was mentally alert at her death at eighty-three years.

There are many well-documented case histories of persons who suffer severe emotional changes at specific time intervals.

Tests have demonstrated that these emotional changes show a relationship to unusual occurrences in the body, such as sudden increases in the quantity of blood cells, recurrent fevers, migraines, or abnormal fluid retention.

In women, the emotional biorhythm cycle shows an approximate 28-day pattern, the same as the menstrual cycle. Although menstruation causes physical as well as emotional changes in the body, these changes should not be confused with other biorhythm cycles.

Biorhythm cycles show that certain illnesses do seem to take place at certain times of the day, as women who have suffered "morning sickness" will be quick to acknowledge. There seems to be a universal rise in body immunities during the late afternoon period, due to peaks in white corpuscle production. This late afternoon "strength" is in sharp contrast to increased *morning* sensitivity to radiation and germs.

Drug studies have yielded startling results on this point. For example, the *same amount* of amphetamine may kill as much as 77 percent of a group of test animals or as little as 6 percent. The result depends entirely on the time of day the drug is administered.

THE SUN'S RAYS AND OUR DIURNAL INFLUENCE

What is it that sets our "clocks" in motion? Most human biochemical changes relate to an approximate 24-hour sequence that is termed the *circadian rhythm*. (This is slightly off center from the precise 24.8-hour lunar day, or the 24-hour solar day, but in harmony with both.) Humans are diurnal, or light-loving, in contrast to nocturnal, or nondiurnal creatures, such as some rodents, bats, and certain cats, who sleep during daylight and prowl after nightfall. Experts believe light waves, penetrating the body through the optic nerve and striking the pineal and the pituitary glands, set off many of our endocrinal activities. This sets hormonal discharges into play which affect a wide range of body activities. Some researchers now theorize that one reason city teen-agers become sexually mature before their early-to-bed country cousins is due to prolonged exposure to artificial lights!

Biorhythm experts have found that matching their own daily habits to diurnal time brings extra energy, even when it means a return to old-fashioned bedtime schedules and early rising. Similarly it has been discovered that the person who is *up* when the sun is down often experiences untimely fatigue.

Studies show that the body requires a steady, rhythmic pattern for smooth, healthy performance. The sick body also mends itself in rhythmic cycles. This importance of clockwork timing in health was amply demonstrated by a series of studies on patients at European health retreats. These studies show that the clockwork regularity of sleep and spa meals, plus strictly scheduled baths and massages, worked to help the body heal itself. A synchronized daily schedule seems to aid in resynchronizing key body organs. For example, those cardiac patients whose heart irregularities showed a six to one arrhythmia with their respiration returned to the more normal four to one relationship. Needless to say, emotional well-being was restored as well.

It is unfortunate that most working people are still entrapped in a nine-to-five work schedule, because more varied work patterns could bring more fun (and fewer traffic hassles). In northern parts of Sweden and Siberia, where the sun shines for almost 24 hours a day in early summer (and barely shows its face in deep winter), round-the-clock office hours, as well as factory schedules, stimulate more biorhythmic adaptability. And when workers are permitted to choose their favorite work times, one notes that even diverse work shifts are filled—and cheerfully manned.

But to survive an extreme changeover in work hours, gradualism is important for health. (The reader may want to refer back to the deleterious stress effect of shifting work schedules, page 36.) The human organism (being highly adaptable) learns to anticipate its work stresses at specific times of day. Thus a normal person requires at least three weeks to adjust body rhythms and insure vitality.

ARE YOU A LARK OR AN OWL?

By nature some of us are larks, while others are owls. This difference in energy levels at different times of the day can have a dramatic impact on relationships, particularly marriage. The wife who is sluggish at the breakfast table may be chirpy and full of fun by nightfall, ready to party when her tired, depleted husband just wants to watch TV and fall into bed. Can you change your biorhythms? Sometimes. But the first step is to discover and restore your true body time.

BODYPOWER TECHNIQUES TO RESTORE YOUR BODY CLOCKS

(1) Go on "free running time" for two weeks. Put simply, this means going to sleep when drowsy and rising without alarm clocks. Seemingly simple, this is best approached with scientific precision: Carefully schedule your mealtimes, shun liquor and drugs (even aspirin), and avoid emotional stress whenever possible. It helps to drink a large glass of warm water just after waking up each morning. Choose natural, easy-to-digest foods, and don't eat between meals. Such natural revitalization brings you a beauty bonus: on "free running time"* you will get more Stage IV REM sleep, smoothing away premature facial lines. If you are overweight or a black woman or past 35, there is one

---

* "Free running time" is the term used by scientists who live in subterranean isolation studies, usually deep, down in the earth. Free of the sun's diurnal influence, they fall into natural biorhythms, establishing a rise and fall in blood pressure, urine volume, hormones, hemoglobin, and other body functions.

thing you can do to make your health watch count for more: buy a blood pressure gauge (a sphygmomanometer) and, with a friend, measure your blood pressure, twice a day.

(2) *Schedule some work task at the same time daily, for two weeks.* Here the woman with a factory job has an advantage (provided she avoids the exasperation that boredom brings). When you expose your physical being to *consistent* work stresses at precisely the same hour every day, it helps to regularize your body rhythms, making synchronization automatic. (Creative excitement, or a job that has its "ups" and "downs" can disrupt harmonious functioning.) You can reproduce this conditioning at home, by doing one of the following at precisely the same hours, for the same amount of time, two hours, each and every day: heavy housework; uninterrupted typing; gardening activities; a brisk, purposeful walk; bicycling; or a shopping expedition. Regular mealtimes and simple foods will also be a help during this experiment.

DISCOVERING YOUR OWN ENERGY WAVES

Once you restore your body rhythms, you will discover real body magic—automatically timed energy waves that can be relied upon to occur day after day. Studies have shown there is a kind of energy wave (in the form of adrenal discharges) around 6:30 A.M.; this is a time when irksome tasks become easier to handle. I have also noted an otherwise unexplained burst of vitality around 5 P.M.* Once you restore clockwork harmonies, these energy surges will be regular and dependable. Such boosts of energy make it easier for a working woman to "hang in there" when tired in mid-afternoon. Anticipating their arrival makes the interim bearable.

---

* As this book was going to press, English medical studies brought documentation for this. In healthy persons, new endocrinological studies show that a high adrenal discharge is seen around 5 P.M. daily also. It might be noted that this is a two-edged sword: it gives you extra vitality for "rush hour" traffic ordeals, but makes you more hostile if aggravated.

Each person's biochemistry is unique. Once your body is restored to orderly schedules, you might discover other energy surges. A socially active friend of mine swears she enjoys a 1 A.M. energy burst, which leaves her fresh and revitalized. (This has irritated several escorts. The perpetually energetic companion can be just too much for the overstressed executive who simply wants a quiet dinner and then home to bed.) Another acquaintance, a young teen-ager, claims she has a 10:30 energy surge that makes sleep difficult. Her solution is a later (or earlier) bedtime.

There are no words in common Anglo-American usage to describe the self-pride a woman enjoys, once she learns she can depend on her energy waves at specific times of day. English must give way to the Japanese *satori*—used by Zen Buddhists to define that rare flash of insight that brings new hope in its wake. This describes the psychic reward one receives, once one learns one can depend upon the rhythms of one's body.

THE 90-MINUTE HOUR, OR ULTRADIAN RHYTHM

Scientists have now discovered that our bodies go through certain 90-minute cycles during waking hours, just as they do in the stages of sleep. This periodicity has been named the *ultradian rhythm*. It affects alertness and particularly influences oral reflexes; these can bring on overweight or excess smoking.

In one study, volunteers were placed in observation rooms that were furnished with a refrigerator containing snacks, a coffee urn, and cigarettes. They were encouraged to spend from six to eight hours doing whatever they chose. They were unaware that a record was kept of each time they placed something in their mouths: food, cigarettes, coffee, even fingers. When their oral behavior was plotted against time charts it was found that they all put things in their mouths at regular intervals of about 90 to 100 minutes. Another test confirmed this, where people spent

36 hours in a soundproof chamber, performing various tasks. They had to press a toggle switch whenever they wanted water and food. Tabulations showed that the food requests tended to cluster, every 90 minutes or so. When brain wave patterns and heartbeat frequencies were monitored, they also showed 90-minute cycles.

Thus oral compulsions and appetite fluctuate at a regular rhythm, a fact that was first established by a pioneer woman scientist in Japan, Tomi Wada. She inserted balloons into the stomachs of volunteers, then recorded the changes in air pressure over a period of hours. In healthy persons, she noted a 90-to-100-minute interval between stomach contractions.

This same ultradian rhythm has been found in frequency and intensity of fantasies. For instance, young males have a tendency to envision sexual scenes—with 100-minute cyclic regularity. This also, quite obviously, is related to attention spans.

What does this mean for women? It has been seen that stress makes such ultradian signals more pronounced. Dieters should be cautioned that emotional problems can make one feel compelled to eat between meals, or at odd hours, or smoke excessively. Persons in critical job situations demanding a high level of alertness should be on guard against mind-wandering every 90 minutes. This also shows that a certain amount of regularly recurring mental fuzziness or mental fatigue is normal.

The sexual aspects of the ultradian rhythm and its 90-minute "hour" are still under study. A psychiatrist suggests that couples of the future might use biorhythms to schedule their times of enhanced sexuality. It works the other way, too. He speculates that the phrase, "I'm in an ultradian trough," might someday replace today's hackneyed "I've got a headache" as a ready excuse for avoiding intercourse.

We're all familiar with spring fever, and the ways in which humans are affected by the changing seasons. According to Arctic researcher and biorhythm scientist Dr. Joseph Bohlen and his equally venturesome wife there is a biochemical basis to seasonal change. They lived among Eskimo tribes for several months during the dark polar night; they wanted to ascertain which body rhythms are independent of solar influence. During each of the four seasons, they visited Eskimo huts around the clock to take urine samples, pulse readings, and other vital statistics from subjects, in addition to testing for eye-hand coordination and hand-grip strength. They found that the seasonal variations caused definite changes in body temperature and in calcium and potassium levels. Living without sunlight brings unexpected calcium upheavals within the human body. During wintry darkness, subjects excrete *ten times* as much calcium as during the light-filled summer. As we discuss elsewhere in these pages, it is known that calcium shortage can bring anxiety and nervousness. Scientists therefore now believe that this calcium imbalance accounts for the seasonal disorder, peculiar to northern climates, called Arctic madness.

Just as migratory birds, seals, and whales react to seasonal urges, so do human beings. Indeed, generations of climatic changes might determine ethnic and emotional differences in people from different parts of the world. Though ethnic generalizations should not be oversimplified, anyone who has observed the stark, penetrating gloom of the Arctic night will agree with those who suggest this contributes to the high suicide rates in Sweden. By contrast, Polynesians and Fiji Islanders on the other side of the world are renowned for their sunny dispositions.

WHAT WOMEN CAN LEARN FROM THE BIORHYTHM ENGINEERS

Biorhythm engineering is accepted in Japan and Switzerland, and is thought to be a sound guideline for safety and increased industrial productivity. It is not unusual to see Japanese workers wearing biorhythm badges. These are different colors to indicate whether a particular day is critical in one of three biorhythms: physical, emotional, or intellectual. Critical days occur when these rhythms change from low to high (or the reverse). When such biorhythm curves cross on an individual's chart, a doubly critical day is to be expected. In Japan, biorhythm charts are considered as much of a safety measure as automobile seat belts are to Americans.

Japanese drivers are now required by law to either learn how to chart their own biorhythms, or subscribe to a computerized service to do it for them. Industrial giants such as Mitsubishi, Asahi Glass, Hitachi, and Tohoku Electric Company have employees charted if they are responsible for the safety of others.

Even among conservative American businessmen, biorhythms are now considered good accident prevention. In a study of 1,000 industrial accidents, it was reported that over 90 percent occurred on a critical biorhythm day for one of the participants. George S. Thommen, Swiss-born biorhythm consultant, says it is not the slow or lazy worker who gets hurt on such days—it is usually the fast and impulsive one. One industrial worker suffered a serious back injury when he lifted a heavy packing case—despite advance warning that such weights should be handled by two. Later he was charted, and his biorhythms revealed that on the day of the accident all key body rhythms were high. Later interviews confirmed that that day the laborer felt so good he was confident he could manage without help.

The pattern of our biorhythms has affected the success of many famous athletes. Mark Spitz was "fated" to set new records at the 1972 Munich Olympics: throughout the week of swimming competition, his chart showed favorable highs in physical and emotional rhythms. When Floyd Patterson regained the world's boxing championship, his biorhythms were at a peak. When Arnold Palmer won the British Open, it was during a week when he was enjoying a triple-high period of biorhythms. Yet he went on to lose badly just two weeks later (to Gary Player in the P.G.A. tournament). It was a rare time of triple-low biorhythms.

PREDICT THE SEX OF AN UNBORN CHILD—WITH BIORHYTHMS!

The sex of your unborn child can be predicted with bio-rhythms. When intercourse occurs at a time of biorhythmic physical high for the woman, she becomes receptive toward cells from the male sperm, and a male is conceived. When the *emotional* cycle is high, a girl might be conceived. It has been found that the physical biorhythm high seems to hail a time of alkaline conditions in the bloodstream; an emotional biorhythm peak favors a condition of blood acidity, experts claim.

As an energy guide, we can concentrate on the 23-day physical biorhythm. (Thommen doesn't regard the 33-day intellectual biorhythm as overwhelmingly influential for most men and women.) The time when vitality is high is during the first half of this physical biorhythm period (11½ days). This is when we enjoy a feeling of physical well-being. This is the period when European doctors who follow this new biorhythm science will schedule operations. It is the time when stamina as well as energy is high, when athletes perform their most outstanding feats.

The day the physical biorhythm crosses the sensitive chart areas and plunges to the last half of the cycle is a critical time, with accidents possible. According to biorhythm experts, this is the period when death strikes the aged or the decrepit. Death charts of celebrities bear this out: examples include the late Duke of Windsor, Pope John XXIII, J. Edgar Hoover, and Carl Jung.

The last half of our 23-day physical cycle is a time for recharging. Rest and convalescence come easier at such a time.

Simple shortcuts for establishing your key biorhythms are given in a chart at the back of this book (page 000). If you find arithmetic to be more of a chore than a challenge, we include a list of sources from which you can order your own chartings.

According to George Thommen there is a quick way to chart your peak emotional sensitivity. This is the 28-day rhythm that determines emotional vulnerability and governs your nervous system. It dates from your birth and runs in an orderly sequence of four 7-day weeks. So if you learn *the day of the week* on which you were born, you'll know that your critical emotional time will repeat itself on the first and the fifteenth days. With the exception of Leap Year babies, the woman who was born on a Tuesday will know that every *second* Tuesday is a time when she is prone to emotional upset or nervous error.

HOW DRUGS UPSET YOUR BODY RHYTHMS

As we mentioned previously, most drugs alter or disrupt our biorhythms; the degree depends on the drug and the dosage. In one experiment, female rats with regular fertility cycles had their biorhythms measured after a dosage of sulfamerazine, a common infection fighter. The subjects normally went into estrus (heat) every 4 or 5 days, and they had regular menstrual cycles. This regularity persisted during therapy, but the subjects appeared strangely animated and active. Sleep was difficult and hunger periods changed. Gradually the estrus cycle changed; then the animals went into heat every 20 to 36 days.

After therapy ceased, reactions were even more disturbing: some animals began to behave like manic-depressives. They would appear hyperactive, then this would be followed by inertia and seeming fatigue. During this time overeating and weight gain became serious health hazards. Vaginal smears showed that hormone discharges were disrupted also. One leading medical researcher suggests that pharmaceuticals may work on the thyroid gland in ways we have yet to discover.

The female hormones estradiol and progesterone have also been studied in terms of their effect on biorhythms. As with the sulfa drug, there were few notable changes during times the hormones were administered, but striking desynchronization was noted after dosage was stopped. Estrogen supplements seemed to trigger some sort of serious disruption of body regularities for nearly *seventy percent* of all subjects tested.

Although menopausal estrogen replacement, or use of the Pill, were not specifically tested, we can learn from this biorhythm research. It has been suggested that when a woman with a 27-day menstrual cycle uses the sequential version of the Pill, it may affect her in different ways from a woman with a 35-day cycle. Prolonged use of the Pill will affect the menstrual regularity of all women. And many versions of the oral contraceptive seem to sacrifice body harmonies for packaging convenience. Searle Laboratories suggests to users of its Dem-ulen product that the first dose should be taken on the Sunday after the beginning of the menstrual cycle, whenever this occurs. For even the most regular woman, this could provoke variations of from one to six days in her biorhythms, month after month.

A BODYPOWER TECHNIQUE TO CHART YOUR ENERGY RHYTHMS

It is predicted that physicians of the twenty-first century will provide us with time schedules and biographs to help us coordinate pharmaceutical doses with other disruptions in body rhythms, such as work changes, time shifts, and jet travel lag. We know already that pain tolerance seems to vary with the clock. Perhaps in the future we will know enough about these biological highs and lows to be able to schedule dental appointments, or facial surgery, at times of maximum comfort; then pain and nervousness will be minimal.

Meanwhile, learning to chart our daily energy swings offers each of us a unique advantage: it brings a feedback of body knowledge, and teaches us to listen attentively to body signals. (It has helped some of us to identify the exact moment of ovulation, thereby turning a joyous new page in fertility control.)

You can set up your energy chart to begin on any day of your menstrual month; most important is to keep your records faithfully, day after day.

Use stars, or asterisks, and each morning rate your vitality with a one-to-four-point system. Women executives can note this on a secret corner of their appointment calendars. The homemaker can improvise a desk calendar schedule. (You will find that this mood chart also becomes a confidence booster.) If certain days bring low energy due to sleep lack, or overindulgence, record this data. Record your observations after no more than a single cup of tea, coffee, or juice; this excludes any false energy rise due to caffeine or nutrition.

After a few weeks, such self-monitoring will help you begin to notice your energy waves as they occur from day to day. And in addition to letting you pace your month, this tally will do much to point out for you the link between energy and emotional calm. When you begin to know when to anticipate energy "highs," you can put more fun (and fitness) into your life.

CHAPTER 10
Sex and Your Energy Levels

It is an unscientific myth that says that the female of the species is less hardy than the male. The majority of women are blessed with superb innate vitality to carry them over the life-depleting hazards of childbirth. Women's natural stamina is also seen in their longevity statistics. Women emerge as the longer-lived sex, providing we avoid the chronic illnesses of mid-life, as discussed earlier.

In itself, a satisfying sexual relationship is considered to be salutary to both emotional and physical health. An excess of orgasms at a single coitus might be fatiguing, but intercourse, in general, builds vitality. Habitual sex also builds libido, and becomes one of the most mutually beneficial addictions a married couple can acquire. Within sensible limitations, frequent sex also can prevent arthritis. Marriage counselors say it builds self-confidence and mutual esteem as well. Masters and Johnson claim that regular intercourse helps a woman avoid menstrual cramps (although posture factors might be involved here, as we shall discuss). All experts agree that mutually satisfying sexual intercourse bolsters mood. As one sex counselor notes: When sex is good, everything in the world looks good. When sex is bad, nothing else is good enough.

Until now, ignorance of the nature of our bodies has led us

103

women to limit our physical activities. This is not necessary, and indeed, can be crippling to both body and spirit.

Women, once called the playthings of sex, have a crowded sexual agenda. First, let's talk about the biggest anxiety of women from 15 to 50—pregnancy—and learn ways in which a woman can control and maintain her sexual resources.

THE PILL, AND OTHER CONTRACEPTIVE METHODS

Worry about contraception can be a real energy-depleter. For many women, the Pill (despite its side effects) offers a reliability that nothing else yet provides. The best way to make use of the Pill is to remember three facts:

(1) There are many versions of the so-called Pill, many with low estrogen amounts and fewer side effects. Be sure to ask your doctor about experimenting, if you're not satisfied with the one you have.

(2) It helps to give your endocrinal system a "vacation." Plan a change to another contraception technique for at least one month every year. Again, discuss this with your doctor. Some women become very fertile when they stop the Pill, but this is usually not until some weeks have passed.

(3) The Pill may make you anemic, for complex reasons. Your best bet: take a daily dose of *ferrous gluconate,* an iron remedy that is available without prescription, costing about two cents a day.

Watch your symptoms carefully. Pay special heed to your blood pressure (the Pill provokes hypertension) and *don't* take the Pill if you're a heavy smoker or noticeably overweight. The Pill has brought paralysis and death by stroke to tense women who were stroke candidates already.

For these reasons, the intrauterine devices (the loop, coil, and others) might be safer. Again, symptoms should be carefully monitored, for all women cannot wear such internal devices. Talk with a woman gynecologist on this if you prefer.

The most promising contraceptive for women (in addition to improved fitting of the old-fashioned diaphragm) is a dandy idea—if it works. Announced in early 1975 by scientists at the Massachusetts Institute of Technology, this is an *under-the-skin birth control capsule.* Because it is placed within the body, it requires lower hormone amounts. Presumably this brings fewer side effects. The capsule itself dissolves slowly in the body, and is constructed of biodegradable materials. Only minor surgery is required to position it, and it reportedly brings no discomfort except at time of insertion (when a local anesthetic is given). Called subdermal capsules, these contraceptives had not been tested on humans at this writing.

Since subdermal capsules are not available to the public yet, and many women cannot tolerate the IUD, I would like to add a few comments on the Pill. Throughout this book, I urge women to take a more decisive hand in their personal medical care. Nowhere is this more urgent than in selecting the right oral contraceptive. In America the steroid-hormone content of leading versions of the Pill ranges from 23.10 mg. per tablet (of *Oracon,* a Mead Johnson product) to 0.55 (for Wyeth's low-estrogen *Ovral*). All prevent ovulation, or they would not be marketed by today's lawsuit-conscious drug companies. Yet many physicians persist in a patient-deluding "bedside arrogance"— they base their choice of *which* Pill to prescribe on whimsical reasoning or haphazard criteria that approach insult.* While many gynecologists are enjoying their self-appointed Pygmalion roles, they are flooding women's bodies with life-draining steroids. They are doing this despite periodic warnings to physicians from the U.S. Food and Drug Administration that the fewer steroids and hormones that are introduced into a patient's body,

---

* Medical journal advertisements suggest using the size of a patient's breasts as a time-saving "femininity test": the smaller the breast, the higher the estrogen dosage in the Pill selected. Does this build bigger breasts? Rarely. The most common result is overall weight gain—and more deadly side effects due to hormone excesses.

the healthier she will remain. And, circumspect doctors agree, the less the estrogen, the less the danger of clotting, strokes, or future cancer.

Lest we level a heavy indictment on the ethical, albeit fumbling, gynecologist, we might recall that Anglo-American medicine is more humane in its attitudes toward women patients than other "advanced" nations.* Indeed, much of the blame for this Pill confusion should be shared by the pharmacist and the woman herself. Neighborhood druggists, shrugging off the need for regular medical monitoring of patients, often slip to favorite customers a few Pill containers without prescription. And some women complain vociferously when they receive a Pill prescription that is limited to a three-month supply, requiring a return medical visit to check for side effects. Dr. Emanuel Greenberg, a New York gynecologist, finds it exasperating that many women refuse to vary their Pill prescription. "I'd rather stay with what I have. I don't want to risk getting pregnant." Patients protest,† rather than agreeing to change their prescription to minimize side effects.

Feminists deplore use of the Pill, and they are right in their disgust with the medical establishment that would continue to subject a woman's body to the Pill's range of side effects. (Now mustache-hair growths are seen on many Pill users, especially black women and those of Hispanic origin—an emotionally depressing mark of endocrinal upheaval.)

However there is no denying the new freedom—with minimal worry—that the Pill has accorded women. Sexual appetites have

---

* In France, the person most instrumental in obtaining passage of a limited abortion law was feminist Gisele Halemi. She tells of a time in her younger days when a French gynecologist took a self-righteous look at her butchered and bleeding body (after an illegal abortion) and decided to give her a curettage without anesthesia, "So you'll never be back here again." More recently, the women leaders of France united to take an advertisement in a leading Paris newspaper. In a nation that liked to *send women to jail* for having abortions, they announced that *each* of them had had illegal abortions: Françoise Sagan, Simone de Beauvoir, and Catherine Deneuve, among others.

† Much latent fear stems from early notoriety about the "Rock rebound effect" —the theory that conception is a certainty once Pill-taking ceases. Gynecologists now find that years of Pill use make it difficult for a woman to conceive readily.

been increased, for the Pill (and the IUD) permit sexual spontaneity, a signpost on the road to true equality for women. According to a Princeton University study, there is a 21 percent increase now in the frequency of intercourse among married couples, compared with just a decade ago. The major factor is widespread use of the Pill and IUDs, which reduce anxiety about unwanted pregnancy. According to a 1974 survey, career drives have also improved. Working women who take the Pill are out sick less than nonusers (an average of 4.7 days a year, compared with 5.6 and more for nonusers). Women report their work efficiency has improved because they feel more relaxed and less concerned about getting pregnant.

But I urge women to persist in their demands for safer, less energy-depleting methods, aimed at giving a woman rightful mastery over her own body. Many medical research miles remain to be traveled before a woman can bear children when and if she chooses—*at no harm to herself or her future.*

MONTHLY CRAMPS—AND BODYPOWER EXERCISES TO OVERCOME THEM

Do you have occasional menstrual cramps? Physicians are newly cognizant of the way poor posture and swayback can bring on simple cramps (called *dysmenorrhea*). If your cramps are painful, see a physician. But if bad posture causes monthly tension, any or all of the following exercises can help. (They also bring sexual rewards, by stimulating blood circulation throughout the pelvic region.) You don't have to perform them all, or many, at one time. Just try them, choosing those that suit you best. If you want to exercise during your monthly period, go ahead; just stop when you feel tired.*

(1) *The Pelvic Rock.* This exercise helps straighten sway-

* Yoga gurus say it helps a person grow in inner strength when she learns to consider fatigue as a signal, pacing exercise according to her body responses.

back. (Caution: do not attempt this during pregnancy.) Do this: Stand with body balanced on both feet, arms lightly crossed at chest. Inhale. As you exhale, draw your buttocks slowly together, and try to tuck them under. During this, firm your lower abdomen. Then draw your tummy forward and up. (This is a slight movement, but wonderfully revitalizing when practiced daily.) Hold this position for a count of three, then relax. Let gravity return your buttocks to their original position. Repeat four times. Practice this twice daily if swayback is a problem.

(2) *The Body Brace.* Stand with your back along a wall, feet three inches from the wall, facing forward. Keep arms relaxed at sides. Now bend your knees slightly and press your back to the wall. Then place your palms against the wall. Try to tuck your hips under, bringing your pelvis forward. Now raise your ribs "up" from abdomen, lifting head and neck as if a pulley were attached. Then relax your arms and stretch to loosen your shoulders. Walk forward from the wall and try to maintain this "tucked-under" pelvis for as long as possible.

(3) *The Triangle.* Stand with your feet about 24 inches apart, arms extended at shoulders. Now *inhale,* bending slowly to your left side. Do not force, but attempt to reach your left ankle with your left hand. While you do this, bring your right arm overhead, bringing it to rest alongside your ear. Now hold your ankle firmly and stretch your body as you exhale. Hold this extreme position for ten seconds. (Think of your legs as an energy triangle, with power rising through them to energize your entire body.) Return upright and repeat to other side.

(4) *The Gluteus Maximus.* This is an easy exercise that can firm up your buttocks. It is marvelous for improving body awareness in one of our most insensitive (and cushioned) body areas. Do this: Stand relaxed, and alternately flex and tighten buttocks muscles (*gluteus maximus*). Activate each cheek twenty times, then pause and activate both together five times. Daily practice (which can be done unobtrusively, at random moments) pays sexual rewards—especially for menopausal women.

(5) *The Fetal Roll.* This easy exercise returns a youthful flexibility to your lower spine. Do this: Lie on your back on

padded carpet or exercise mat. Inhale deeply while you bring your right knee toward your chin. Touch knee to your nose, if you like (but don't force). Exhale as you return leg to floor. Repeat with your left leg, inhaling as you coil your body into the roll, then exhaling as you unwind. Now bring both knees upward and inhale; again exhale as you return to outstretched position. Repeat twice, or three times if you feel supple.

(6) *The Reverse Posture.* This is a simple exercise—a yoga position (or an *asana*). It might be a bit strenuous for older women, but it builds majestic body control. Make sure your head is cushioned and practice this no more than one minute at a time for the first week. Do this: Lying on back, raise both legs gracefully to a right angle, upward from the floor. Place your hands under buttocks for support, thumbs under your hipbones, elbows only 12 inches apart on floor. Keep your knees straight but relaxed, and point your toes. Now close your eyes and practice abdominal breathing for several seconds. Then relax and return feet to floor. When practiced daily, this yoga position rejuvenates sex glands and thyroid activity. Because of its toning action, it can slow the aging process.

THE MENOPAUSE: PROBLEMS AND RENEWALS

Never has there been a more opportune time for a mature woman to enjoy and develop her life. While there is more stress to complicate our mid-life changes, there are new ways to ease it. Society now respects a mature woman for her own merit. No longer is her prestige based on whether her father, husband, or son was a civic leader, or whether she even had a father, husband, or son.

The decades for love and romance have been extended. "Ageless" charmers can meet and, now, marry the handsome younger men of their dreams. Such December–May relationships work out quite well, such as the marriage that has prospered for over forty years between actress Ruth Gordon and author Garson Kanin, sixteen years her junior. Merle Oberon's spirited grace can laugh at the passage of time; so does her adoring, decades-younger bridegroom. The Dinah Shore–Burt Reynolds relationship has brought zest and enrichment to both their lives for a significant period—for no longer is a woman socially condemned if she chooses not to marry. Yes, this is an era of free-form relationships and serial marriage, where love can blossom again —and again. Romance has become a matter of energy and mutual interest, and is not restricted to the young.

Elizabeth Barrett Browning (herself some years older than her poet-husband) dismissed the social complications of this older woman/younger man phenomenon with easy tact: A woman is always younger than a man of equal years.

This brief statement, however, overlooks two traits that remarkable women throughout history have shown. Whatever their country or callings, most of these extraordinary women became more successful after maturity than in earlier decades. And each refused to let the menopause play a significant role in her life.

The French language offers a good idiom for the menopause. The more enlightened French describe this period as *le retour d'âge*, or "a return to the youthful years"—those carefree times before the responsibilities of fertility.

THE SECOND PUBERTY

It is said that we humans have a particular curse: we are aware we are mortal. Self-consciousness about aging may be why so many women fret and aggravate themselves into making the menopausal changes frightening—and energy-depleting. It is often the hard-working, lower class woman who eases into her post-menopausal years. She makes active use of her body—and has little time to worry. Highly successful women such as Estée Lauder, Agatha Christie, Golda Meir, and that perpetual ingenue

Carol Channing had more pressing priorities, so they found menopause easier than their less-busy contemporaries. When I asked Eileen Ford, the glamorous modeling agency tycoon, about her own menopause, she shrugged. "I can't remember when it started, and I don't know when it stopped."

What happens, exactly, at menopause? It is a time of endocrinal changes just as puberty is. From puberty to the menopause there is a glandular rise and fall, much like a balanced seesaw. Most of these peaks and drops are triggered by the ovaries, and they are controlled by the all-important pituitary gland. In what is usually an orderly sequence, the ovaries secrete certain hormones. These release an egg for fertilization and prepare the womb for the fertilized egg, or fetus. If conception does not occur, a kind of housecleaning takes place in the womb. This is a frantic (and energy-consuming) cycle. The fact that it ceases after the age of 50 can be a blessing. For, after a usually brief* transition period, a woman can enter her finest, most personally fulfilling hour, as we shall soon see.

How do health and endocrinal harmony continue, once the ovaries shut down? This can be understood with one simple biological law: the pituitary is central to all endocrinal changes —and the pituitary remains active until death. Physical (and emotional) fitness determines the degree of pituitary response. But even when the ovaries cease to produce hormones, the pituitary signals the adrenal glands to step up estrogen production.

Some specialists in women's medicine claim that estrogen production *increases*, at least for a time, at menopause. I went to Australia to interview Dr. William Griffith McBride, whose long-term menopause research† is highly respected by medical

---

* Gynecological surveys show the average menopause lasts between 15 and 18 months. Many women have no symptoms or health problems. As one busy socialite said, "I just realized one day that I hadn't had a period in over a year."

† The McBride research also shows that the menopause occurs later than heretofore: Most healthy women retain their ovarian function until around the age of 51.

men on all continents. He told me he had discovered that many women enjoy an upsurge in estrogen for six months after menstrual periods cease. As a natural body adaptation, this eases them into the post-menopausal years.

What about estrogen supplements? Dr. McBride agrees with those gynecologists who say that fewer women need hormone supplements than is believed. Women who seek out a gynecologist for menopausal treatment are the ones with bothersome symptoms; yet of these, *less than one out of two* requires estrogen drugs. The reason for such a conservative medical 'attitude is this: excess hormones can be as hazardous as insufficient hormones—and sometimes more so.

The typical woman needs only a minuscule amount of hormones for good health. In terms of estrogen, throughout a lifetime, the average female body produces *less than one-fifth of an ounce* of estrogen and progesterone combined. And a woman's body maintains estrogen production (from the adrenals) for a number of years after menstruation ceases. According to landmark research at the University of Buffalo Medical School, well over 55 percent of nearly 1,500 women continued estrogen output for decades after menopause—some as long as fifteen years after, and many in markedly generous quantities.

Excess hormones are destructive, according to endocrinal studies by Dr. Hans Selye and others. Estrogen, in particular, threatens the female body in two ways: (1) Excess estrogen is cancer-flaring; and (2) excess estrogen, like other drugs, must be destroyed or detoxified in the human liver. (Overworked and, in some, malnourished, the liver is called the body's chemical factory, for it must cope with pollutants, food chemicals, and various intrusions on the body—in addition to nearly 500 other duties.) Beauty damage results once the prematurely aged liver is placed under extraordinary stress. It neglects such responsibilities as vitamin storage and enzyme production, and cripples the production of new skin cells.

The American drug industry now spends an average of $3,000 on every gynecologist every year, persuading him to press certain drugs on his patients, especially estrogen. Thus it is mostly American doctors* who will dash off an estrogen "cure" for such borderline menopausal symptoms as anxiety, insomnia, depression, fatigue, and headaches.† With the known dangers of excess estrogen—especially in an aging body at a time of heightened cancer susceptibility—this is short-sighted and cavalier, to put it kindly.

Yes, estrogen can offer relief from the hot flushes during menopausal change—we do not question this. (Heavy anesthesia also brings oblivion from childbirth labor.) But it is debatable whether the hot flashes are due to waning estrogen. And a woman's endocrinal network is a system of delicate balances. Injected hormones can disturb glandular interactions; under certain conditions such intrusion can *diminish* adrenal estrogen manufacture.

There is one symptom that might be estrogen-treated, but it usually occurs in post-menopausal women (ages 60 and over). It is a drying up, or atrophying, of the vaginal mucosa. This is the vaginal fluid that serves as a lubricant during sexual intercourse. For men, too, advancing age can diminish the amount of seminal flow as it does the vaginal fluid. But before suggesting the extreme remedy of estrogen supplements—ingested by mouth and therefore circulating throughout the body—cautious physicians prescribe hormone ointments. Estrogen is among the most easily absorbed of all steroids. An estrogen ointment, locally applied, requires only minute hormone amounts. And just as an IUD offers fewer side effects than the Pill, so the topical application of hormone ointment is less threatening to overall health.

Critics of estrogen therapy feel that, although estrogen might not initiate the cancer spiral, it *is* a contributor to hastening it along. While direct cancer causes remain the subject of much controversy, the thoughtful woman should not risk becoming another cancer statistic. For there are alternatives, and less risky

---

* See back-of-book Medical Bibliography for medical reports from other nations, including Norway, Germany, and Argentina. Recent estrogen warnings have also been issued in the United Kingdom and the *European Pathology Journal*.

† These "symptoms" might not be caused by endocrinal imbalance, and would best be referred to a medical specialist in a nongynecological field. With laudable exceptions, most U.S. gynecologists find it difficult to pronounce Galileo's brave words: "I do not know."

therapy.* Even when estrogen is given temporarily (during the handful of months of menopausal changes), it can be phased out gradually. In recent research,† doctors found that estrogen supplements remain in the body for three days after ingestion. So doses need only be given on *alternate* days. They found that in most cases, the best approach is to reduce estrogen amounts every five years. When the prescribed quantity was given at age 55, it was lessened at age 60, then again at 65, and so forth. By comparison, Ayerst Laboratories, American makers of estrogen supplement "Premarin," suggest keeping a menopause patient on estrogen therapy for the rest of her life, however long (or short) this might be.

There is another less-publicized estrogen side effect—listlessness. The spayed-cat personality of the woman taking estrogen supplements is the antithesis of what is admired in our vitality-conscious era. Preferring to sit on the sidelines of life, such women gain weight readily. This further depletes their once-youthful energy and enthusiasm. Such patients, it is reported, are more docile about medical care‡—and one wonders if they are not sedated out of self-determination and ambition as well. As one fitness expert likes to remind this overmedicated generation: Rome was not built by a tranquilized Italian.

BODYPOWER ENERGIZERS FOR THE MATURE WOMAN

When a woman is forty and over, her body has unique reactions and mood changes. The following techniques will bolster

* In Europe, menopausal treatment can range from iron injections and folic acid nutrition to exercise and physical therapy. It is not unusual for a personal physician on the Continent to recommend a spa visit for body rejuvenation. A vacation at Baden or Montecatini thus becomes tax-deductible, beauty treatments included.

† Dr. McBride's research in Australia.

‡ Estrogen patients are "easier to manage," promises a tape recording sent to American gynecologists in 1974 by Ayerst Laboratories.

your control of your body. They are easy, and two of them can be performed wherever you are. One helps you keep at peace with yourself. The others will offset fatigue by summoning up reserve energy when you need it most.

(1) Most adult women don't get enough calcium, iron, and certain B-complex vitamins. You'll avoid anemia and boost nervous control with this simple Bodypower *cocktail*: Add 2 tablespoons of brewer's yeast* to a large glass of tomato juice. Stir thoroughly and drink slowly. (This acts as a beauty tonic as well, because it boasts anti-gray hair nutrients.)

(2) Whenever you feel your energies are prematurely depleted, reach for inner reserves. You can do this by stimulating your upper leg arteries, which connect directly to the heart. Most of us don't use our bodies enough, so if you're healthy and of normal weight, do this: Find a convenient corner (in a public washroom, if necessary) and do twenty kneebends.

   OR

Walk up a flight of stairs.

   OR

Take a brisk walk around the block. Stretch your upper leg muscles as you walk, and breathe from the lower abdomen.

(3) When you feel yourself becoming moody or upset, try my favorite yoga breathing exercise. (It is called *pranayama* by gurus.) Do this, wherever you are: Sit quietly. Then place your right forefinger on the right side of your nose and inhale. Hold breath briefly, then move your right finger to close your other (left) nostril. Exhale air through your right nostril. Alternate nostrils this way for five leisurely breaths, inhaling through one nostril, then exhaling from the other. This little exercise works miracles at soothing endocrinal upheaval and avoiding many self-destructive upsets.

---

* Brewer's yeast is a powdered supplement available at all health food stores.

MID-LIFE ENERGY BOOSTERS

Don't rationalize about fitness. A famous American TV actress once told me she had no need for exercise. ("I walk to the newsstand to get my papers instead of having them sent.") Three months later she suffered a nervous breakdown that cost her both her husband and children.

Do analyze your boredoms. *Anomie* has been cited as a common sickness among housewives—"that bored feeling of purposelessness . . . felt as the problem that has no name." Once a clever gal faces up to the fact that her life is no longer filled with events or sparkling people, she has cleared the decks for action: she can consider ways to renew herself and her lifestyle. As one of the principles of yoga states, many problems carry with them their own solutions.

Don't overvalue holidays. Much mid-life depression comes from building up your expectations for an upcoming holiday. This creates a slump when your birthday is forgotten or there's no New Year's Eve party. A better idea: Stop waiting for the phone to ring—give your own party!

Do find ways to improve your willpower. Self-discipline practice helps keep you youthful, said Nobel-award-winning rejuvenator Dr. Alexis Carrel. One Broadway actress maintains year-round discipline by keeping her bi-weekly exercise appointments, rain or shine. Try this discipline with nutritional benefits: At the same hour daily, eat a cup of cottage cheese. Taken at 5 P.M. such a protein snack curbs hunger. It also helps the social drinker avoid cocktail excesses.

Don't curtail your energy by old antagonisms. In years of journalism, one of my most surprising interviews came from an older woman heading a Washington government agency. She assigned mature women to Peace-Corps-type work in urban areas. I asked her why she never assigned volunteers to work in their own cities. "Why, in their home towns, their old enemies are present!" Curious as this may seem, it makes good sense. Is there a tradesman or a neighbor whom you avoid because of some ancient disagreement? Have you crossed a street to avoid meeting somebody recently? If such fences can't be mended, consider a new neighborhood.

Do try a personal time-motion study. A record of exactly how you spend your day reveals much about wasted energy. A noted stress consultant to industry says: Some people don't realize they are spending two hours a day on the telephone, discussing yesterday's trivia.

Don't be shy about seeking expert help. Advice for widows, retirement planning, biofeedback training for migraine sufferers, hypnosis for smokers, dieters' groups, and other counseling can now be found—at budget prices.

Don't waste time with "gloomy Gussie." Some people take a perverse satisfaction from comparing troubles. When talk becomes a "downer," recognize the source, and avoid it.

Do find a cause and support it. No matter how young you are at heart, it is putting your ideas into action that leads to true renewal. As Alfred North Whitehead said, "The vitality of thought is in adventure. Ideas won't keep! Something must be done about them."

Don't indulge in coffee if you're nervous or arthritis-prone. Feisty octogenarian Dr. Max Warmbrand (who has cured thousands of arthritics with nutrition) warns that coffee sets up toxic blood imbalances. Eventually this might lead to joint inflammation.

Do watch your weight. During mid-life your metabolism slows down. If eating habits continue unchanged, overweight always results. This opens the door to mid-life disorders such as hypertension and diabetes.

Do make ideas more important than possessions. Moving your residence every few years has an advantage: it forces you to weed out trivia. Musty memorabilia can be comforting, but it will weigh down your progress. As William James observed, "Lives based on having are less free than lives based on doing or being."

Don't engage in "cold potatoes talk." At the Esalen Institute, experts suggest a unique theory—"Energy" discords are set up in the atmosphere of a room where people sit around, murmuring things they don't really feel. Meaningless chatter can lead to ennui and inexplicable hostility.

Do add faith to your "survival kit." The woman who believes that extraordinary things can happen is more fun to be around than a hard-eyed skeptic. Especially at mid-life, there are emotional health (and cosmetic) benefits from a faith in man's universal brotherhood and goodness.

Don't lie. This is an important key to inner power. It can be self-crippling to murmur soothing untruths. Yogis believe lying depletes will and self-determination. Even Socrates advised that false words infect within as well as without.

Do make an effort to control your thoughts. That woman who notes her mind drifting into stormy or depressing emotional waters will enjoy more energy if she directs her thinking to more pleasant subjects: a hobby, her last vacation, her next one.

Don't be an exercise dallier. Scientists at the University of Maryland have proved it takes at least three steady exercise minutes for oxygen to be boosted into the bloodstream. At mid-life, fitness proves a priceless beauty treatment; it provides a woman with collateral that nobody can take away. Years after the Broadway success of "Mame," I interviewed the real Auntie Mame (Mrs. Ruth Tanner, once of Buffalo, New York). She had endured incredible economic loss and was penniless at age 65. Never embittered, she stood majestic and straight as an arrow. Daily yoga exercise since the twenties had brought her peace of mind, and a poise that the world's most expensive cosmetics could not duplicate.

Do take risks. Many mature women become too afraid of failure to dare the unknown. Ex-astronaut Michael Collins says that each time anyone is offered an option that he or she doesn't accept, something inside that person seems to die a little. Courage can be built up gradually, like a muscle, often in the face of fear itself. And it has to be exercised, even during a time of great success. In a newsmagazine profile, the award-winning film director Francis Ford Coppola admits, "I was terrified of [making] *The Godfather.* I was terrified of *The Conversation.* But I want to keep rocking the boat. Taking chances is what makes you strong, and makes you wise."

Don't forget to smile. It is not a coincidence that unhappy women have mouths that turn down at the corners. Long a mental health rule, pretending to be in good spirits will soon perk you up. A sense of humor brings its own excitements. Walt Whitman, sensing this, dedicated *Leaves of Grass* to "Life immense in passion, pulse, and power—cheerful."

Do learn the art of emotional transference. Most of the emotional problems for mature women can be traced to family situations. The new breed of family psychologist will interview a whole family if one has an emotional difficulty. (Personal interactions can provide clues to the problem.) When one loved one brings upset and anger, learn to transfer your good feelings, at least temporarily, to another. This provides a rewarding outlet for your bruised ego—and an emotional climate in which it can heal.

A BODYPOWER TECHNIQUE FOR MID-LIFE TENSIONS

More than at any other time, mid-life exasperations can create tensions in a woman's body. Doctors say this often accounts for unexplained fatigue at the end of a day. Deep-rooted muscular tension is wasted energy. But body awareness can release those tensions and bring new vitality.

Learn about yourself this way: At least once every day, surprise your muscles. "Freeze" your body into whatever position it has assumed at that moment (at work/shopping/driving your car/riding a public bus). Don't move a muscle, and breathe carefully. Now take an inventory of the way each part of your body is behaving; especially notice the way you are holding parcels or a handbag. Is your back stiff? Are you holding a pencil or shopping bag with unnecessary tension? Are you crushing your underarm bundles with extra force? If you are seated, are your thighs taut? If legs are crossed, are your knees mashed together? Is your jaw clenched?

Some persons have discovered that they buckle their toes, unconsciously. Or that a shoulder is held tense and rigid. One fastidious woman found that she unknowingly arched her fingers. A man learned that he was stroking thumb and forefinger in an energy-wasting tic. Only you can notice where, and how much, tension you are creating. Eventually such tension can give birth to muscular deformities. On a day-to-day basis, this can ruin your mood as well as your body, as we learn in Chapter 15 (The Psychophysical Techniques: New Ways to Ease Your Tensions).

CHAPTER 11
Nutrition for Bodypower

Nutrition is an obvious and important source of energy. But there is much confusion today about the amount of nutrition found in popular foods. So before we discuss what foods can do for you, let's consider what they can do *to* you.

Before his death from stomach cancer in 1974, British actor Laurence Harvey commented in an interview: "What is most absurd about my contracting stomach cancer is that for years I have discriminated carefully about what I ate. I always made it a point to select only the finest food and the very best wines."

That statement was twice saddening to those of us who knew him. For it is indicative of a prevalent myth among many affluent people that nutrition is the same as expensive cuisine. We now know that certain cuisines (especially spicy foods, such as Szechuan, Mexican, and Korean) can be deleterious to digestive health unless these foods are accompanied by simple, easily metabolized foods at the same meal.* In many civilized lands, peasants enjoy more energy-building foods than do millionaire industrialists in big cities. Worse, urban executives endure more

---

* History's pages abound with success stories of persons who bypassed *haute cuisine* for the sake of vitality, among them Augustus Caesar and Napoleon Bonaparte. Even after the acceptance of gastronomy as the chic French national pastime, Napoleon scorned rich delicacies. He explained that his future was more important than culinary tidbits.

stress, make less use of their bodies, and are exposed to a wider number of contaminants.

Modern man (and woman) still has the caveman's liver: few evolutionary adaptations have occurred since the days of uncooked meats and wild herbs and honey. American and English stomachs, especially, are not genetically conditioned for highly seasoned, rich foods.* Carbohydrate pastries and overcooked meats, consumed at the same sitting, over a period of months can ruin digestion. Even the classic French cuisine, however pure the ingredients, muffles vitality, for it depletes energy by a kind of gourmet Gresham's law. Especially for the person who is over 35 (or who works under stress), the aging stomach gradually loses its ability to secrete complex digestive enzymes. This is seen in an inability to form those pepsins required to break down whole milk or citrus. This is why some persons feel gassy or flatulent after drinking orange juice. Other adults find it easier to digest skim milk than high-fat whole milk. Chronic use of hard-to-digest foods can deplete body energy; this is most noticeable during those hours following mealtime.

THE GREAT DEBATE: DEVITALIZED FOODS AND CANCER

The causes of human cancer are diverse, varying with temperament, heredity, and lifestyle. And it requires elastic criteria for scientists to directly link nutrition to stomach cancer. Officially, the American Cancer Society denies any cause-and-effect relationship—yet privately they note that countries with highly seasoned foods as part of the national diet, such as Korea, show a high incidence of rectal cancer.

---

* Uneven digestive abilities might be hereditary also, says Dr. Roger Williams of the University of Texas; this could account for variations in vitamin absorption from person to person (and nation to nation). "A nutritional deficiency can occur even when an individual consumes food containing enough of the nutrient in question." This might be due to faulty digestion, or malabsorption of the needed nutrient through the intestinal wall.

New, disturbing questions have been raised by the American Health Foundation. Their nutritional scientists now link meat-eating with cancer incidence. A 1974 A.H.F. study showed a relationship between American meat-eating habits and the growth of anaerobic bacteria. The latter are suspected to lead to cancer of the colon. One medical survey cited the fact that a vegetarian sect, the Seventh Day Adventists, showed a singularly minor incidence of cancer (colon, pancreas, breast, prostate, and kidney) when compared with other residents of the same state.

Although most scientists avoid any anti-cancer claims for vitamin A, recent research suggests that this vitamin can boost natural immunities. Among its partisans is Dr. Umberto Saffioti, of the Chicago Medical School. He boldly states that vitamin A prevents carcinogenesis (formation of cancer) by increasing the body mucus protection. Dr. Martin Zisblatt, an independent researcher, agrees this vitamin helps mobilize body defenses, especially against breast cancer. His work suggests this is due to the role of vitamin A in postponing aging of the thymus gland.

A recent development in medical practice has been the recognition that the integrity of the body must not be tampered with except in cases of extreme and urgent need. Consequently, certain medical therapies now are referred to as "intervention"; drugs are described as "chemical intervention"; emotional therapy is "psychiatric intervention." An important question which has been raised about physiological integrity is whether or not it can be destroyed by the intervention of food chemicals.

Some medical researchers say suspicion of food chemicals is nonsense. Others insist that a diet high in refined foods and chemical additives can be energy-depleting.

A few stout-hearted biochemists, braving the scorn of their peers, point to one indisputable fact: food chemicals are market-tested in a manner that refuses to question their total effects. There is little testing to determine the *interaction* of chemicals either within the stomach or as they combine within refined foods. There is also a shocking lack of study to determine the long-range, cumulative effects of nonessential additives such as mono-sodium glutamate. Critics of food processing have turned this debate into the most heated controversy in nutrition today. Chemical additives accumulate within the body, claim natural food advocates. It has been noted that thirty-five years ago cancer, hepatitis, and other viral diseases were rare. This was a time when food produced for human consumption contained few, if any, synthetic chemicals. Today viral diseases are not only a commonplace, but they are increasing at an alarming rate.

It is outside the purview of these pages to discuss whether refined foods can age or deteriorate the human body. Suffice it to say that the cautious consumer can shop for foods containing a minimum of chemical additives. In addition to known brands that are advertised as being based on pure ingredients, health food stores offer new options; such natural foods are free of chemicals and carefully labeled.

HOW TO INCREASE YOUR VITAMIN ABSORPTION

In addition to avoiding energy-depleting food, the knowing consumer will consider habits that can increase her absorption of those nutrients present in whatever foods selected. The following will bolster your body resources:

(1) *Keep your feet warm.* Natural medicine experts, such as Dr. Max Warmbrand of Orlando, Florida, say that keeping your extremities cozy while dining aids digestion and improves vitamin absorption.

(2) *Only one protein at each meal.* Especially for persons over 35, heavy protein strains digestive faculties. California's Dr. Henry G. Bieler claims that the human liver is incapable of handling two proteins at once. So the solar plexus, or abdominal brain, gets busy and chooses one of three ways to avoid stress: (a) the meal might be vomited; (b) stomach muscles might let only one protein pass into the small intestine for digestion, while they retard the second—an energy-depleting digestive delay;

(c) faster digestive muscular motions, or peristalsis, might be set up. This results in diarrhea.

(3) *Use no salt.* That's right, sodium chloride upsets the body's mineral balance. Many physicians now say that table salt interferes with uric acid elimination; this can aggravate eczema symptoms and foster arthritis. All cardiologists advise against salt: it is a known factor in hypertension. And as any once-pregnant woman knows, salt is a major contributor to weight gain. Salt needs are filled by regular servings of raw fruit or vegetables, both replete with natural salts. If you are a die-hard user, druggists and health food stores sell salt substitutes.

(4) *Six foods only at each meal.* This is a tough rule to follow (especially around buffets and smorgasbords), but such caution pays high energy dividends. We'll skip the gruesome descriptions about the way the lower stomach can come to resemble one huge garbage heap. Just agree that many foods at one sitting might trigger a digestive delay, and sometimes bring distress. Spare your digestive enzymes and they'll reward you—with after-dinner energies.

(5) *Mealtime serenity.* Ulcer experts and gastroenterologists emphasize the importance of agreeable dining conversation and emotional harmony. (One pioneer in psychosomatic medicine proved that the stomach lining becomes inflamed during stressful emotions. Obviously this threatens digestion and vitamin absorption.)

(6) *Start kitchen vitamin protection.* At the world-famous Bircher-Benner Clinic in Zurich, nutritionists say that kitchen hygiene is critical to vitamin preservation. Sneezes, coughs, or uncovered arm scratches must not be permitted when food is being prepared. If the cook suffers from the sniffles, use of a surgical face mask is essential to preserve nutrients, especially during salad preparation. Also, the kitchen should be well-lighted: vitamin-destroying bacteria thrive in dark, unwashed corners.

(7) *Use lemon in salad dressings.* European experts claim there is medicinal value in certain foods, particularly the citric

acid in lemons. When the juice is used over raw vegetable salads, it offers wide antibacterial protection. Also, raw onions and garlic provide "antibiotic" values helpful in warding off early cold symptoms.

(8) *Favor garden-fresh vegetables.* There is natural vitality, or life force, in vegetables that are grown without insecticides or chemical fertilizer. Also, fruits and vegetables provide stronger nutrients when served within hours of picking. (Even when stored in the shade, spinach can lose nearly 80 percent of its vitamin C content after 48 hours). Sunshine wilts carotin, the vitamin A factor, as well as depleting B vitamin content.

(9) *Cook lightly, if at all.* Vegetables and fruits offer extra nutrition when eaten raw. Another vitamin saver: learn to pare lightly and discard little. Trimming vegetable skins can cause a vitamin loss of nearly 30 percent. Other guidelines: remember that the outer lettuce leaves are richer in nutrients than pale, inside leaves. Young cauliflower and kohlrabi leaves offer high carotin. The more vivid the color (tomatoes, carrots) the more enriched the nutrition.

(10) *Beware fruit storage.* Fruits are high in acid content; peeled, they should never be stored in metal containers, which sometimes leach. Transfer fruits promptly from glazed dishes or earthenware, also.

(11) *Use suitable cooking utensils.* Use wooden spoons for cooking and stirring; nickel, silver, and other metals might corrode from contact with strong acid foods, especially apples or sauerkraut. Fireproof glass is a very useful kitchen container, as it does not contain metals that combine with food chemicals.

SMOKERS' NUTRITION—AND CHLOROPHYLL

In America there is still a certain disdain for nutrition among physicians. So to learn the most medically advanced techniques for using nutrition to energize and heal, I journeyed to Europe.

There I interviewed physicians at the aforementioned Bircher-Benner Clinic in Zurich. This is where aristocrats and heads of state repair when their energies, and spirits, are depleted. (Patrons have included Gloria Swanson, Haile Selassie, Henry Ford III, and noted European industrialists.) This establishment uses nutrition as a medical tool, and prescribes foods the way Anglo-American doctors prescribe drugs. Founded in 1902 by the late Dr. M. Bircher-Benner, this family-owned retreat scorns the word "spa" in favor of "clinic," so doctrinal is their belief in the curative power of nutrition. One of their theories involves the use of chlorophyll, found in all green, growing plants. This natural factor, they believe, promotes red blood cells, fights anemia, and improves circulation better than most iron therapy. Frequent use of raw foods is prescribed as a way of increasing microelectric "tensions" within body cells—and thus releasing new energy.

One of several medical consultants to the clinic's nearly 70 patients emphasized that an orderly daily schedule also helped ailing bodies heal themselves. At Bircher, the typical day begins with 6:30 A.M. rising, which most patients follow with a walk in the rose garden. At breakfast, the highlight is the famous Bircher *muesli,* a combination of nuts, grains, and fruit.*

Coffee is not permitted (nor is alchohol or cigarettes), and animal meats are never served. The clinic believes that vegetable protein is less hazardous, and healthier than animal protein. Also, in most of the countries of the world today, meat is filled with antibiotics and hormones. Eggs are available at the clinic but not recommended.

After post-breakfast relaxation, the patient begins an individually prescribed round of herbal baths, sitz baths, massage, and the unique one-hour toning shower. Gymnastics are scheduled for certain patients, featuring special neck exercises to counteract stress and release tension. (See Chapter 15, The Psychophysical Techniques.)

---

* So puristic was the Bircher head chef about his *muesli,* that he courteously refused to give me a sampling at 11:30 A.M. Prepared two hours earlier, the "biological content" would have altered.

The tasty Bircher bread, a special mix of whole grain flours, is available at all meals. Yet it is the organically grown vegetables that provide the greatest interest. I sampled several and the taste compared favorably with cuisine in the world's noted gourmet restaurants. Made without additives or meat stock, the soups and purees are superlative.

The kitchen planning at Bircher is impressive: dishes are individually prescribed for each patient, and food values separately charted. (One patient might be hypertensive, another overweight; others have diabetes, gall bladder, arthritis, cardiovascular problems, or even cancer. All are treated with naturally grown foods.)

And what is prescribed for energy-building? They give foods rich in folic acid, for instance, as well as iron. These are backed up by B-complex foods and vegetable protein. "But first," one of the medical consultants told me, "I examine the patient to exclude any disease that might be causing the fatigue." A psychological examination follows, aimed at diagnosing any environmental factors that can bring on exhaustion. "Family, work problems, social relationships, marriage problems, perhaps—all these are energy influences."

Daily eating habits at home also are considered, and a complete food history is taken, charting each patient's eating routines —at work, at parties, watching television.

If the patient is a cigarette smoker, a serious discussion ensues. "Heavy smokers tire more easily than nonsmokers," says Dr. Joho, an attractive young doctor at the clinic. "Smokers have more CO_2 (carbon dioxide) and nicotine in their blood. They also are more likely to become addicted to drinking."

Nutrition prescribed for smokers includes vitamin C supplements, to repair the damage that smoking does to blood vessels. Folic acid is also important, and is given via natural foods as well as in vitamin form.

Her complexion aglow despite little makeup, the serene Dr. Joho flushed with outrage at mention of one American medical trend. "Computerized medicine?" she scoffed. "Here, we stay current with nuclear-medicine developments, of course. But we feel a diagnosis must *grow* between a patient and physician.

"There are things one can't find in a computer . . . Here we try to build a confidence, as a friendship you might say, with the persons who come to us."

In itself, retreating to any health clinic or spa can relieve stress buildup. It makes a change of diet easier. "Most patients need separation," she suggested. "It breaks the rhythm of a hectic professional life."

CAN MENSTRUAL FLOW REVEAL POOR NUTRITION?

For some women, the color of the menstrual flow can betray a nutritional imbalance from their daily diet, American nutritionists report. When a *bright red, profuse, odorless flow* is accompanied by uterine cramps, the blood contains toxins that are acidic. They result from chronic eating (or improper digestion) of sugars and starches. These acids have been insufficiently oxidized; therefore the body must rid itself of them by unusual channels.

If menstrual flow is marked by blood that is *dark, clotted, odorous,* and *stringy,* it can indicate that protein putrefaction toxins are present. An excess of meat protein can put the digestive machinery into imbalance. Or normal dietary protein might be insufficiently digested. The most notable odors are caused by eggs, overcooked meats, and cheese.

This is not to imply that every menstrual flow is replete with digestive byproducts. But more and more, enlightened physicians consider that menstrual pain is a symptom that is worthy of investigation, instead of a nuisance to be sedated or smothered. Menstrual cramps need not be woman's sexual lot, to endure without complaint or reasonable explanation. But menstrual symptoms *can* be a useful barometer of your general health.

TEN FOOD-POISONING HAZARDS

Food toxins are another body ravager, and the person who dines away from home is especially vulnerable to salmonella, botulism, ptomaine, and other forms of food poisoning. It is estimated that more than 8,000,000 Americans suffer severe digestive upset each year from toxic food. Such sickness is frequently misdiagnosed, or dismissed as a vague "24-hour virus."

It helps to patronize reliable and reputable restaurants. However, changing labor conditions*—and limited manpower for public health inspection—have been unable to halt this rising incidence of sickness, and the fatigue that lasts days afterward. Vending machine food, seasonal banquets, and questionable highway diners are given but cursory federal inspection, when at all. To avoid the energy depletions of toxic food, beware the following:

(1) *Caution: potato salad.* Low-grade mayonnaise is a warm weather hazard. Used by commercial caterers, it breeds bacteria when left unrefrigerated. Also, when potatoes are boiled, then set aside, they become a contamination ground for proteus bacteria, especially in summer. Important: boil potatoes just before using. Never save potato salad overnight (particularly if raw onions are included).

(2) *Caution: raw shellfish.* Unethical fish suppliers can use sodium nitrate to hide rotting fish odors. Smoked fish can be mishandled in ways that encourage salmonellae growth. Typhoid, infectious hepatitis and other serious diseases have been spread by oysters and clams harvested from polluted waters. Important: buy from established sources.

(3) *Caution: ham sandwiches and egg salad.* So-called ptomaine picnics have been caused by ham or roast beef sandwiches spread with cheap butter or mayonnaise, then left unrefrigerated. Egg salad, too, must be refrigerated between preparation and food consumption.

---

* Food poisoning at one of Manhattan's leading hotel dining rooms bedded me for nine hours during a recent social season. The culprit: Hollandaise sauce that had been allowed to stand too long in the overheated kitchen.

(4) *Caution: holiday hors d'oeuvres.* Many caterers become lax about employee hygiene, just at a busy time when colds are frequent and disease resistance low. Important: Beware of meat hors d'oeuvres; they should be scrupulously refrigerated to avoid staphylococcus.

(5) *Caution: meat gravies.* When permitted to cool slowly after cooking, meat gravies are breeding area for spores of *C. perfringens,* a toxin that brings severe stomach cramps and diarrhea. Important: beware lazy cafeteria heating of beef gravy during summer, when radar heat is kept low for employee comfort.

(6) *Caution: vending machine soda.* Syrups and sodas leave residues within vending tubes that contaminate. Defective soda valves let carbon dioxide back up into copper-coated areas, causing chemical interactions. Important: patronize machines that vend soda in cans or bottles rather than mixing it on-the-spot.

(7) *Caution: candy machines.* For all ages, unwrapped sweets and chewing gum are a health hazard. (These bacteria carriers are no longer legally permitted in England.)

(8) *Caution: drooping salads and warm cream.* When cole slaw is wilted or salad leaves droop, pass them by. This betrays salad leaves that have been left unrefrigerated. Warm cream (unless heated by request) can reveal that temperature codes are not being enforced in a restaurant kitchen. Drink your coffee black, or request *cold* cream.

A BODYPOWER TECHNIQUE TO COPE WITH FOOD POISONING

If you find yourself the victim of food spoilage (and professional help is unavailable), follow this antidote which is effective and much safer than many drugstore cure-alls*: Drink one

---

* Many doctors feel today's patent medicines and digestive remedies subject the liver to added stress. For diarrhea, natural medicine physicians suggest a food that restores the ecology of the digestive system: yogurt.

to two large glasses of warm water (boiled, then cooled). This will dilute the toxins in your digestive tract. Then go to bed, eating nothing until your appetite signals you are hungry. This is glandular rest; it allows the overworked liver an opportunity to detoxify the contaminated food.

FOOD ADDITIVES AND THE "CAVE MAN'S LIVER"

There are now over 3,000 chemical food additives in casual commercial use, and testing of their interactions is spotty. In 1974 Lenox Hill Hospital warned of the human adaptation hazards that are brought by today's omnipresent food chemicals. "In the past we faced the problem of food spoilage. But that was solved. Now we have synthetic foods, which contain chemical ingredients that can cause allergic and toxic reactions."

Dr. René Dubos, award-winning Rockefeller Institute scientist, notes the way man is increasingly being forced to cope with his environment: the human body must do this in ways it is not conditioned to do without stress. The increasing incidence of cancer and cardiovascular disease shows, he says, that some bodies have failed to adapt to these contemporary encroachments.

Food chemicals today can lengthen the shelf life of grocery goods—but they might be shortening our own. What happens when we continually force our bodies to cope with an onslaught of synthetic chemicals that cannot be absorbed or metabolized? Dr. Dubos foresees one drastic outcome: a gradual erosion of the senses and our esthetic talents. He warns that unless present trends are modified, we are doomed to "an atrophy of our uniquely human attributes."

TEST YOUR NUTRITION I.Q.

State whether the following are true or false.

(1) Cheeseburgers build ready energy, for mature women especially.

(2) Lemon juice in salad dressings can build body immunity against disease.

(3) Light-colored lettuce leaves are rich in nutrition.

(4) Cigarette smokers need no special nutrition.

(5) Potato salad is an energy-builder, any time of the year.

(6) Raw vegetables or green-growing herbs foster digestion when served as a first course.

(7) Women on high-protein diets can have a clotted and stringy menstrual flow.

(8) Salt is a questionable seasoning for the busy woman.

(9) Vitamins A and E should be taken together.

(10) Strawberries refrigerated in earthenware will maintain their biological content.

(11) A multi-vitamin tablet daily is adequate for nutrition needs for most persons.

ANSWERS TO TRUE/FALSE NUTRITIONAL QUIZ

(1) False. When served with marbled meats (such as beef or ham) cheese brings a digestive depression. For some, it can cause diarrhea, especially when ingested by persons over 35, or subject to emotional stress. If you're fatigued or busy, take your proteins one at a time.

(2) True. Good any time, lemon's citric acid provides anti-bacterial protection. Idea: brush teeth, or use sugarless gum, after consuming; citric acid is strong enough to erode tooth dentin.

(3) False. With few exceptions, in vegetables, the darker the color, the richer the nutrients.

(4) False. Vascular damage needs to be repaired. Use vitamin C and folic acid, found in liver, wheat germ, and uncooked green leaves.

(5) False. Unrefrigerated potato salad is the most common health hazard.

(6) True. A vitality boost any time, raw vegetables, and herbs

like parsley or mint, can stimulate enzyme production. As appetizers, they ready the digestion for foods to follow.

(7) True. Prolonged, high-protein diets will disturb body metabolism (and age one prematurely). Some doctors feel *overcooked* animal proteins (steak, ham) bring intestinal putrefaction—and eventual arthritis.

(8) True. Especially if you are overweight, a black woman (or suffer from nervousness), salt disturbs body mineral balance; it may bring hypertension. Iodized salt is a rare exception, but useful mostly in areas with iodine shortage, such as the Great Lakes. (Such residents show a high incidence of goiter, which some nutritionists attribute to iodine shortages.) But the most reliable iodine is that obtained from seafood or natural iodine supplements. When salt is added in cooking, less is better than more.

(9) True. Most useful in the form of alpha-tocopherol, vitamin E improves vitamin A absorption. You can also increase absorption of iron by taking vitamin C. Nutritionist Dr. Shelia Callender suggests drinking orange juice to sharpen the nutrition from your breakfast eggs. (As a cautionary note: never take iron and vitamin E together. At least six hours should transpire between such supplements for maximum absorption.)

(10) False. Keep fruits in glass, never metal, earthenware, or plastic.

(11) False. Vitamin pills cannot substitute for the nutrients in food, they only can supplement. It is debatable whether the aging body, especially, will absorb *synthetic* vitamins with the same ease with which it can benefit from vitamin-rich foods.

CHAPTER 12

Body Weight and Bodypower

There is one consolation that the overweight woman now has: most of her friends are overweight, too. One out of every three Americans over 15 years old is noticeably overweight.

There are several reasons for this creeping mantle of overweight. In addition to new eating habits (and more eating of "junk foods"), television has greatly changed our leisure time. Daytime hours, entire evenings, and weekends can be spent in the sedentary situation of watching television. And snacking is a natural companion to television viewing.

Wider use of convenience appliances in the home also deprives us of easy opportunity for weight control. Grandmother used to keep trim by sweeping, hand-washing clothes, and rug beating.* She climbed stairs in a larger house—helping her make regular use of her total body. Today's woman is confined to smaller quarters—and when she goes outdoors on errands she uses motor transportation instead of walking.

The change in contemporary living also includes new mealtime emphasis. In previous decades, and in agricultural societies, the midday meal was the big meal of the day. Thus our bodies

* Television viewing uses a mere 61 calories an hour. Housekeeping routines once consumed over three times this, about 185 an hour. They also provided a chance to work off emotional tensions.

had time, and opportunity, to work off calories, after we consumed them. Now the evening meal is an occasion for prolonged family socializing, and overeating. (Medical studies show it is those calories that are consumed after 7 P.M. that contribute most to body fat.)

These societal trends have become self-perpetuating in another way: obesity runs in families. In America, fifty percent of fat persons had two parents who were also heavy. Eighty percent of the "fatties" had one parent with weight problems. Overweight is doubly dangerous when it develops early. This is because body cells of fat children develop what is termed *adipose-perpetuation*. A high fat cell content (however health and energy depleting it is) comes to be the natural condition of such bodies. These dieters physically suffer after crash diets, for their cells are not appeased until that lost weight is restored.* Keeping the weight off is so difficult, it can be likened to a form of torture.

How does this knowledge help the weight-conscious woman? If you were an overweight child, a gradual diet is your best bet, for keeping weight off will be as tricky as losing it. Quick-weight-loss diets should be avoided: they will bring nervous tension and emotional upset, during the time your body cells are adapting. You should also avoid an equally fattening habit: one-meal-a-day compensatory eating, known to obesity experts as *gorging*. A sure-fire way to gain weight, single-sitting excesses seem to throw body signals into a turmoil that upsets the metabolism. In its own way, gorging contributes to the self-deceptions that bring about dieting failures. ("I'm entitled to an extra goodie at the dinner table. After all, I went without breakfast!")

Studies show that one-meal-a-day eating (and overeating) changes the biochemical makeup of our cells,† much like the

---

* Among obesity experts, this problem is known as the "yo-yo syndrome." It marks many dieting failures and it can bring self-loathing to persons who cannot understand why they eat compulsively.

† In one obesity study, one group of lab animals was fed once daily, a second group was given free access to food. Cell analysis later showed the eat-when-hungry subjects had a skin cell content of just 7.8 percent fat, balanced by 22.4 percent protein. The overeaters ran their fat content up to 23.6 percent, with a low 17.4 percent protein.

childhood obesity we discussed earlier. In addition the hypothalamus does not function properly; this cripples the all-important satiety center of the brain. Even in normal persons, it requires from six to nine minutes for the body to signal the mind it has had enough. Chronic overweights do not seem to receive such signals. They just keep eating until sheer bulk brings digestive discomfort.

One-meal-daily eating also increases your body production of lipids (leading to atherosclerosis), and it strains the liver. Nutritional scientists warn that once adapted to a one-meal-daily eating pattern, body changes tend to perpetuate it: overeating becomes a habit. This is why some obese persons find it difficult to limit themselves to the small portions that most weight-loss diets recommend. (By comparison, we note that just as gorging desensitizes the metabolism, medically supervised *fasting* seems to aid in its recovery.) Dr. Roger J. Williams, medical researcher at the University of Texas, offers this sound advice: "We have heard obese people boast that they eat only one meal a day. If so, this may be the very worst regimen for them to follow. Five or more [judiciously chosen snacks] . . . would be vastly better."

FIRST NATIONAL DIETERS' ENERGY SURVEY

Every woman who is overweight knows, deep down, that she is depressing her energies. I wanted to learn more about the boundaries of this, so I went to some qualified experts, successful dieters. With the help of the Diet Workshops, a cooperative of over 900 diet clubs, I surveyed dieters in 38 American states and Canada. Several facts emerged from the responses to our detailed questionnaire.

(1) Most overweight women gradually cut down on their outside activities. Few realize how minor a role they come to play in everyday life—until they reach the point of becoming an obese recluse.

(2) Most women still lack the self-confidence it takes to diet because of a dare or a bet (as men can do).

(3) Overweight women in our society reach a complex state of self-hatred and self-pity. This makes it difficult for them to become aggressive in making job changes, attaining a satisfying sexual relationship, pursuing educational goals, and other ambitions.

(4) There is a special hazard period for dieters, between three and four every afternoon. Midafternoon fatigue makes it tempting to go off your diet at this time.

(5) Fat persons often explain their overweight by claiming they have a unique glandular condition that makes it impossible to keep the weight off. This is not medically justifiable. Less than one percent of these persons suffer from such a physical condition.

(6) Most overweight persons make half-hearted attempts at dieting for years. For instance, they eat low-calorie ice cream, or "diet" candy, but their daily calorie total remains the same.

(7) Successful dieting improves the body's response to internal signals. It also sparks sexual renewal.

Today most diet doctors caution their patients against expecting miraculous life changes once their ideal weight is achieved. For depression follows on the heels of great expectations, and a disappointed woman will return to overeating. Our dieters' survey brought an abundance of success stories, however, many of them from mature women who had almost given up hope for fun and excitement. In Boston, Massachusetts, Clare A., a sales executive, was delighted to find that her life became more eventful as pounds began to disappear.

"My night life changed," Clare reported, "because I couldn't sit around at night and eat and watch television and stay on my diet. I had to find other things to occupy my time. I went shopping at night, visited friends and family."

Then, as her confidence returned, she widened her world into newer social circles. She became active in volunteer work, the P.T.A., and a local Camp Fire Girls group. "I started doing things I had always wanted to do," she said, "but had been too self-conscious about my weight to participate."

Why did she wait so many years for this self-realization? "I feel most of my fatigue was on an emotional level, low self-esteem, and all of the feelings that go along with it."

With new energies freed, many successful dieters look back and realize how they closeted themselves away from life. Donna S., a Wilmington, Maine, secretary, said, "I think I used fatigue as an excuse for not being seen by thin people." One 42-year-old Illinois housewife told a memorable story about how her extra poundage became a personality burden. And no wonder—back in 1950 she was a contestant for Miss America. But that was before marriage, housework, and six children boosted her weight to 236 pounds. Midway in her diet (after a loss of 56 pounds), she was surprised at the extra energy she had.

"I can hardly contain myself some days, I feel so energetic, or high on life, that there are hardly enough hours in the day to complete all I want to do." She once hated to wake up in the morning and now she sleeps so well she is "ready to go before the sun is up, sometimes." Her description of the way the over-weight mother learns to sacrifice for family and loved ones provides a special insight into the "causes" of overeating. "I had developed patience and tolerance; so much, in fact, that I lost my own identity as a person because their needs were always first." It got so that she never ventured an opinion in conversations. "After all," she remembers, "who thought of a *fattie* as having any abilities at all?" Her self-loathing increased, for she felt tired all the time and especially in the evening. Sex had become a real chore. "Now it's a beautiful experience that I look forward to."

Similar personality changes were seen by a Diet Workshop member in Adams, New York. In her early thirties, prior to dramatic weight loss, she dreaded household chores and her house was a mess. She still doesn't feel wildly enthusiastic about household drudgery; but now the house gleams and she has the energy to make many of the family's clothes as well as draperies and slipcovers. Before dieting she was physically inactive, her feet hurt constantly, and an old knee injury was getting worse with every pound she gained. Today she bicycles and goes sledding with her daughter. What's more she has decided to start mechanics' school. She announces firmly, "I can hold up under anything that comes my way," adding, "somewhere along the way I have gained a very high survival instinct."

Homemakers find that the cycle of boredom-into-snacking-into-overweight makes obesity an easy downhill slide. The kitchen is always handy and usually nobody is around to catch you nibbling. (One women's reporter noted that it was easy for Jacqueline Kennedy Onassis to keep chic: She never had to prepare a child's lunchbox, and, later, face the temptations of half a peanut butter sandwich or a leftover vanilla cookie.)

For the homemaker, overweight makes household routines even more humdrum. One Kentucky housewife, Joyce S., found herself displeasingly plump at only 28 years old. Now, after substantial weight loss, she realizes the way she started to "favor" her body bulk by limited activity, setting the clothes hamper on the stairs, for example, rather than taking clothes up promptly and putting them away. When any exertion makes you puff, you get lazy. Obviously, limiting body use brings on still more weight gain.

The new sensuality that almost all of our 110 respondents revealed points up one key aspect of our survey. Our printed questionnaire included the following question: *"Now, as opposed to the 'old you,' do you discover that your mind is more responsive to body signals, reactions, and cues?"* It was my theory that, as fat melted away, such physical renewal might unblock various networks of body communications, such as satiety cues, et cetera. Forty percent of our successful dieters now find that summer weather is not as troublesome—adaptability is easier, because body cells are toned. A massive weight loss by a Midwestern dieter, one Joyce S., 33, brought the ability to appreciate minor temperature changes: "I'm cold when it's cold and hot when it's hot—not neutral, like before."

I did not ask whether it was easier to achieve sexual orgasm after weight loss, but some dieters hinted that this was the case. A Bellevue, Washington, housewife, Madelynn C., only 30, recognized that her own insecurity as a "fattie" made her supersensitive and sometimes hostile to others. Now she feels good about herself, "so other people seem so much nicer and more understanding." She postscripts, with quick candor, "Now I feel much more 'sexy'—and enjoy it, too!"

BODYPOWER AND MITOCHONDRIA

Each of our 110 survey respondents noted that the fresh energy she found after dieting was surprising—and gratifying. Are there other reasons for such renewal, in addition to weight loss?

It is my theory that successful dieting acts to revitalize a tiny but all-important link in the body energy network, the mitochondria cells. These tiny cells, whose existence had not even been established in 1950, are crucial to the transfer of energy at the cell level. Right now they are being researched at the National Institutes of Health in Bethesda, Maryland. According to Dr. Vincent E. Price, special assistant to the director of the Institute of General Medical Studies, N.I.H., a full *20 percent* of the official U.S. Government medical research now relates to body energy. He told me that priority has been given to mitochondria study.

So small that five *trillion* mitochondria will fit into a teaspoon, these dynamic cells are considered the source of 93 percent of our body energy. Dr. Price predicts that mitochondria will become a household medical word within a few years: "Today's talk is about cardiovascular diseases. The next 'generation of diseases' will be mitochondrial diseases."

CHAPTER 13

Behavioral Conditioning for Easier Dieting

As we have seen, extra poundage can drag down your energy as much as it ages your body. Fortunately, there are easy techniques now available to help you diet—by changing those habits that brought on unwanted weight.

Behavioral conditioning (as these techniques are termed) offers extra reinforcement for dieters going through emotional problems. What I call E-T-M, or eating-through-misery, will put weight on many women as fast as pregnancy. Therefore, one leading diet doctor, Philadelphia's Dr. Willard A. Krehl, says that psychology is all-important in weight loss. He gives would-be dieters a detailed questionnaire to fill out before he will accept them as patients. It is a subtle quiz that helps to strengthen dieting willpower—by putting them in touch with their true feelings about themselves.*

Some of the most famous research on overeating habits was done at Columbia University. Scientists found that, for complex reasons, overweight persons are more responsive to outside food cues than people of normal weight. Tempting aromas, colorful

---

* A sample question: "Do you really want to reduce?" Dr. Krehl says this is a key point, for many dieters are not convinced, deep down, that they are really fat. Such wobbly motivations can weaken the desire to remain on a dull, austere diet.

advertisements—all whet the appetites of people who are already overweight. This preoccupation with food leads to between-meal eating, as well as extra difficulty in staying on a diet.

A complicated and self-destructive spiral, this condition is one that overweight persons despise, yet feel helpless to resist. This leads to self-loathing. (But as we learned in the last chapter, this can be turned into a new pride-in-self, once a dieter succeeds in turning her life around.) It is imperative for mature women, especially, to rid themselves of extra weight, for reasons other than the physical ones. According to obesity studies at the University of Texas, those who are chronically overweight develop fixed opinions and lifestyle habits—what psychologists term *cognitive rigidity*. This can make you uneasy about changing strongly held opinions and make adaptability to changing circumstances quite difficult. It will also hasten the return of unwanted pounds after a successful diet, because you have gotten so used to "favoring" your body you are crippling your chances for a more active (and youthful) life. Such "mental sets" explain why most obese people continue to think of themselves as heavy, long after they have lost weight. (Says one dieting expert: "If an obese person develops a body image or an attitude that he is overweight . . . he tends to be locked in that position.")

But there are ways you can modify your thought patterns, and condition your habits to work for you instead of against you.

DIETING AND EXERCISE: A ROAD TO SELF-MASTERY

As we discussed earlier, if you begin a rigorous exercise program just as you start to diet, you may be asking too much of your body and emotions. However, *gradual* exercise plays a helpful role in our diet drama; it boosts self-confidence as well as beauty. In terms of your appearance, toning exercises will act as a gentle skin massage. (It is important for dieters to restore skin elasticity to the neck, upper arms, and thighs especially.

Our Bodypower Exercise Sequence, page 76, does this. It will also smooth the unsightly "turkey neck," a post-dieting beauty problem for mature women.)

Another major contribution that daily exercise brings to dieters is that it bolsters body awareness and self-determination. Practicing the same exercise, day after day, at precisely the same time, will strengthen willpower, even for those persons who have trouble staying on a diet.

And although our Anglo-American culture has been blind to this, there is a link between the disciplines of athletics and philosophy and the building of extraordinary powers, including psychic growth. Esalen Institute's Michael Murphy likes to cite the example of Tibetan monks, who are assigned *lung gom* walks, lasting day and night for hundreds of miles. When maintained at a steady pace, this physical endurance builds emotional stamina. It helps the monk reinforce his self-mastery and control over his inner life. It is a sure and certain step to build "holding power" for your diet by maintaining a daily exercise ritual, mild though it might be at the outset.

Indeed, physicians are increasingly urged to write an exercise prescription with every diet, according to the president of the Association for the Advancement of Behavior Therapy. Exercise improves a dieter's self-concept. It heightens mood and builds optimism about the future.

Such attitude reinforcement is all-important to problem dieters. Surveys show that the average dieter's resolution seems to die off *after five days* of dieting.

BODYPOWER WAYS TO CHANGE YOUR EATING HABITS

(1) *Don't eat "by the clock."* Rid yourself of the conditioning that lets clock time influence your appetite. Within reason, eat only when you get hungry.

(2) *Do be aware of food proportions.* Fat people tend to unconsciously overeat tasty food. Then they eat less of low-preference foods that might offer more nutrition.

(3) *Don't gorge at meals.* One medical study found that over-weight people eat longer—and hence eat more. Fat people also eat faster, because they are intent about food. Those of normal weight engage in a variety of noneating behaviors at mealtime (putting the fork down repeatedly, talking with gestures, et cetera). This discourages gorging.

(4) *Do make mealtime a diet game.* One diet therapy group encourages its members to put their forks down between each and every bite. They are counseled to use smaller dinner plates, making food portions loom larger. Distractions such as music, an elegant dress, and a pretty table decor can also help.

(5) *Don't eat on the run.* Food gulped or eaten standing up seems to go directly to weight gain, rather than for energy. (Look at the people who walk down the street eating ice cream or hold-ing pizza. Most of them are at least ten pounds overweight!)

(6) *Do chew gum in midafternoon.* As our dieters' survey showed, the "zero hour" for dieters is 3 to 4 P.M. At that time, a piece of sugarless chewing gum can distract from hunger pangs; it will also relieve stress buildup.

(7) *Don't grocery shop when hungry.* Goodies are tempting any time, especially when appetites are high. Try to fill your tummy before you load your shopping basket.

(8) *Do use butter or margarine at breakfast.* Fat stays in the stomach longer than carbohydrates, thus avoiding midmorning hungers. Another good dieting bet is protein. Both are fun to include at breakfast. (Studies show the highest energy regimen consists of a major meal daily—at the breakfast table—made up of high-protein foods.)

(9) *Don't eat the first course.* Especially in restaurants, be wary of appetizers. Most live up to their name and stimulate the taste buds for extra food to follow.

(10) *Do start a calorie-feedback chart.* This technique works wonders at reconditioning your behavior: For five days, keep a

daily (and honest!) list of the food you eat. Tally exactly what, when, and how much you eat. This will pinpoint those hours when you seem most susceptible to nibbling, and help you grow in awareness of other hunger cues and conditions. It also helps you think of your dieting day as a whole. This is important, for many overweight people come to live one meal at a time.

(11) *Don't fill up on gourmet delicacies.* Somehow simple foods are more filling. Gravies and sauces, especially, provide extra calories, empty of nutrition.

(12) *Do consider your diet motivations.* Dieters maintain more enthusiasm for short-term dieting goals (getting in shape for a pending vacation, an upcoming party, a new lover). Long-range plans, such as general health, are admirable, but so vague they make it easier to cheat.

(13) *Don't get discouraged.* Stomachs vary, so does taste. Diets that work for some might not work for you. Keep at it until you find a nutritionally balanced diet that you can stay with. My own favorite: the D-E-A-M-W-F Diet, or Don't Eat Anything Made With Flour. (Breads, cakes, gravies, macaroni, pizza, and so forth.)

TEST YOUR DIETING SENSE

State whether the following are true or false.

(1) You are weight-conscious. You like to study and discuss various diets and dieting organizations.

(2) For snacks, you select only low-calorie colas and diet foods.

(3) For your midmorning coffee break, you always use a sugar substitute and prefer your Danish pastry without butter.

(4) Whenever you're dining out, you find that an extra cocktail helps distract you from menu temptations.

(5) You're nervous when dieting, and seem to be thinking about food constantly. You think that perhaps some people are better off with a few extra pounds.

ANSWERS TO DIETERS' QUIZ

All statements should bring a "false," or "no" answer—except the last one. Here's why:

(1) To make your next diet more effective, don't talk about it with others. (There is a yoga maxim: silence strengthens motivations.) You may become a "diet dilettante"—and conversational bore.

(2) Who are you kidding? It is sedentary TV watching that is considered responsible for America's big overweight problem. Don't nibble when you're lounging around.

(3) Between-meal pastry is silly for a dieter, present or would-be.

(4) Liquor calories are known as "carbo-cals." Among the most dangerous for dieters, they are converted directly to body fat.

(5) You might be right. Research in Israel (and by famed U.S. obesity expert, Dr. Hilde Bruch) shows that chronic dieting can push some people into serious emotional problems, including schizophrenia. It is self-defeating to seek an unreal goal—inappropriate to your body structure and heredity. Instead of attempts to copy wispy fashion models, find the weight at which *you function best* (in mood as well as energy); then aim to maintain that as your special goal.

CHAPTER 14
Emotions: Enough to Make You Sick and Tired

Knowingly or unknowingly, the woman who lets her emotions get the better of her is robbing her energy reserves. Now scientists have discovered that many of us harbor secret mind/body tensions. Even for those persons who are seemingly well-adjusted and "normal," such emotional scars can bring unexplained anxiety and depressions—as well as untimely fatigues.

The woman whose husband struck her during a family argument, the rape victim, the woman whose childhood was marked by stress and poverty—all these women might be unconsciously carrying emotional trauma in their body tissues. Like forgotten bullets, still embedded after old gangland wars, these "tissue memories" remain, disturbing the bearer unawares and blocking her energies. Even if these emotional scars are not troublesome enough for psychotherapy, they are tiring to all.

Today's new breed of psychotherapist (most of whom prefer the term "emotional illness" to the less-curable "mental-illness") recognizes that emotional hangups will block body energy. It is also believed that certain emotional problems, such as anxiety, can start in the misaligned (or misused) body. This is a Wilhelm Reich concept. It holds special meaning for a woman, who is by nature closer to her body than a man. In *They Became What They Beheld*, Ortega y Gasset is quoted as observing that this is a difference between the female ego and the male. Man has inner sensations that remain muffled and somewhat vague. He often forgets about his body entirely, except at times of extreme pain or pleasure. But woman's attention is continually fixed on her inner sensations. We are more aware of our bodies, considering them as interposed between our psyches and the outside world.

Once this body/mind harmony is disturbed, the door is opened to psychological problems. In time, such a "split" leads to neurosis, psychosomatic illness, colitis, ulcers, indecision, depression, chronic fatigue, and, in curious ways, to overweight and obesity disorders. But when body/mind responsiveness is balanced, new confidence results. This brings calm that can nourish and reinforce both the psyche and one's physical being.

Many more women than men are under psychiatric care today.* Inside or outside of hospitals, the largest number of schizophrenics and chronic depressives are women. According to the U.S. National Institute of Mental Health, 68 percent of the psychotics and manic depressives in state-controlled hospitals are women. In private care, 67 percent of the schizophrenic patients are women.

There are promising interactions between body and mind, and Reich's followers have taken separate but parallel paths to examine this idea. Some, like Israel's Dr. Moshe Feldenkrais and California's Ida Rolf (who gave her name to Rolfing) claim that elaborate physical exercises can "realign" one's emotional outlook. The kingpin of this new psychophysical world, Dr. Alexander Lowen, the developer of Bioenergetics, recognizes that such body awareness therapy has a relationship to traditional Chinese medicine. (In Asia today, breathing exercises are part of every convalescent regimen, aimed at restoring inner harmonies.) All agree that physical and emotional links should be scrutinized as a preliminary diagnosis for emotional disorders. A few practitioners go further: Bioenergetics' Dr. John Pierrakos claims to be able to "see" tension trauma as distortions in a patient's energy aura!

---

* This might be due to the fact that male emotional disturbances take other directions. According to statistical studies by Ziegler and Phillips, men turn toward alcoholism, drug addiction, and socially assaultive aggressions, such as rape and robbery.

EMOTIONAL DEPRESSION AND
BIOENERGETICS

Depression is the psychological albatross that casts a periodic shadow over the lives of women. At puberty, a girl soon becomes as familiar with "the blues" as she does with her own menstrual cycle. Indeed, recent endocrinal studies show that, for some, they interrelate. After childbirth, motherhood can be deprived of many of its spontaneous joys by postnatal depression, a manifestation of the triumph of body over judgment. At menopause, emotional depression can deprive even the robust woman of her exuberance and *"joie de vivre."* For the elderly woman, the shock of aging can bring new pitfalls of gloom.*

Intimately known to us all, depression attacks some women more than others. These victims of depression are increasing; in a recent year (1972) there were 230 million prescriptions written for tranquilizers and psychoactive drugs, mostly for women.

Dr. Alexander Lowen says there is a direct link between the absence of energy and depression. Depressed patients complain frequently about energy depletion, and observers agree that the patient's complaint is valid. Even personality and drooping facial muscles show this absence of vitality. The depressed face droops and the skin sags, as if it no longer has the energy to maintain its skin tone. Even the normal animated play of facial movement (eyes, mouth, brow) is absent.

Lowen suggests that energy depletion is related to a low oxygen intake. Over years of psychiatric practice, he has noted that emotionally disturbed persons begin to breathe more shallowly. Early treatments in Bioenergetic therapy work to improve breathing habits. According to Dr. Lowen, his unique exercises increase energy by restoring "a flow of bodily excitation."

Bioenergetics exercises rely on knee-bending; Lowen feels that the locked-knee position (common to most depressed people)

---

* The transitions of age may be strenuous for women in those societies where girls are brought up to consider themselves as sexist "love objects." Where outward appearance is a criterion for womanly status, the wrinkled face and loss of figure can be a demoralizing daily reminder of lost youth.

is a rigid body response to emotional stress. Torso-drooping exercises also try to put patients back into touch with their bodies. For the person who is "well-grounded" is usually decisive, well-centered and stable.

A unique theory sets Dr. Lowen and his Bioenergetics therapists apart from others who espouse this body/mind approach: Lowen finds there is psychological gain in an ability to, literally, fall relaxed. Many emotionally disturbed persons have a repressed fear of falling, even a few feet. This is an inhibition similar to their emotional inability to cry when they are upset.

Certain Bioenergetic exercises symbolize the surrender of one's body to the earth, token of life itself. Lowen likes to remind his followers of the myth of Hercules and his struggle with Antaeus, son of Mother Earth. With the power to regain his strength whenever he touched earth,* Antaeus would spring up with vigor whenever he was knocked down by Hercules. (On the verge of defeat, Hercules realized the secret of Antaeus' power. He defeated him by holding him high in the air, then brought death by strangling.)

In Bioenergetics, once a patient has overcome what is described as an acquired resistance to his body, he learns to release physical tension. This is a secondary symptom of emotional depression. Then the patient is better able to cope with problems as they occur. (Lowen says that "the inability to breathe freely under emotional stress is the physiological basis for . . . anxiety.") †

As a civilization, we are keyed up continually to meet crises. Explains Dr. Lowen, "If a person can't find a natural way to

---

* Lowen's ideas sound poetic, but they result from many years of hard experience with thousands of patients. "It is the living force in the soil which passes into the bodies of all plants and animals. If this force fails us, then neither intellect nor will can insure our survival," he notes.

† This belief is similar to the "fight or flight" syndrome, proposed by Harvard's noted physiologist, the late Walter B. Cannon. Modern man, he suggested, carries the primitive compulsion to engage in combat when antagonized, or else is instinctively driven to flee to safety. Such behavior is discouraged today, but the instinct remains. Thus a day spent in stressful situations (or hostile encounters) will give birth to rigid body tensions. Unrelieved by exercise, these eventually bring tension headaches and "bad" backs.

let down, through his body, he will be tempted to use drugs or alcohol. If he does not let down naturally, he will find himself cast down, sooner or later, into depression."

As an outlet for these repressed feelings, Bioenergetics patients are encouraged to kick a chair or table leg, sometimes shouting "No!" simultaneously. He feels that emotionally disturbed persons acquire a reluctance to say "no," often when they wish to do so. (Compare the comment of New York psychiatrist Dr. Theodore Isaac Rubin: "The further a person gets from expressing his natural feelings, the more neurotic he becomes."*)

Bioenergetics is not bound up in ironclad traditions regarding the role of sex in a woman's life. They state that if there is a time in a woman's life when she is out of sex completely, that, too, is all right.

The thrust of Bioenergetics is on opening up energies. Energies can animate a patient's life, making all problems easier to solve. A typical energy-into-action case was that of a woman in her late twenties. Described as a "total failure" in traditional female roles, she hated to wear dresses and hated office jobs. She had been in analysis for years—it hadn't helped much. Said Miki Kronold, Bioenergetics therapist, "We feel that aggression in a woman should be no less valued than in the male, so we helped this patient open up her natural energies. After a few months, she left her office job and took a job as a cabdriver. She began enjoying sports, went horseback riding more often. Eventually, she went back to finish school. When these other things came together for her, she found a boyfriend."

Dr. Lowen understands the way body misalignments serve as stand-in for suppressed feelings. The neurotic, afraid of his own fearfulness, will exaggerate a pseudo-courage to the rest of the world; he often throws out his chest in bravado, with sucked-in belly and tensed, squared-off shoulders. Interestingly, persons

---

* This book is too limited a context for a discussion of the degree to which many women have twisted their psyches through an acceptance of woman's passive role. Many studies have been done on the relationship between female "passivity" and low self-esteem, poor job performance, and emotional illness.

who have difficulty in discerning personal relationships often develop optic myopia. (Lowen: "Personality disturbances are characterized, not only by some loss of function, but also by a loss of the awareness associated with the function.")

Lowen feels denial of the body leads to a loss of energy and chronic depression. Energy exhaustion is brought about by an impulsive person in other ways: he discharges his energy wildly, thus avoiding feelings.* For some persons, a denial of the body is a way of avoiding hurt and disappointment; it echoes their rejection of normal human needs for love.

Bioenergetics is serious business, and the reader is cautioned not to wander into a Bioenergetics group to make new friends, or because she is lonely. Some patients are deeply disturbed; others are intently preoccupied with self. Patients can include women who have given away their children, call girls making too much money to give up prostitution, or political refugees who have had horrors imprinted deeply on their psyches. And linking such an unlikely assembly of persons are the bizarre groans and twists of Bioenergetics exercises! Such a spectacle reminds a visitor of a surrealistic Fellini or Antonioni movie.

I commented on this to a New York Bioenergetics therapist, Bill Johnson. "You should have seen the group I led just before the last Jewish holiday," he replied. "After the exercises, I told them to crouch on the floor in whatever position they felt comfortable. And as we say during many Bioenergetics sessions, 'Let whatever wants to come out of you, come out.'

"As if from nowhere, there suddenly began the most eerie wail I have ever heard. First by one and then by another, it was taken up, until almost all present in the group of ten were twisting and wailing in some tribalistic agony. The remaining group member looked at me oddly, as if to say, 'What in the hell am I doing here!' "

---

* Such a person, says Lowen, "becomes irritable to avoid feeling his anger, hysterical to avoid feeling his sadness, and promiscuous to avoid his sexual feelings . . . He runs before he is afraid, he cries before he is hurt, and attacks before he is threatened."

Was it a weird scene?

"It was all from another planet! But, after a few minutes," he reminisced, "I wanted to get down on the floor and join them!"

GESTALT THEORY: BODY SIGNALS BRING EMOTIONAL AWARENESS

Gestalt theory is another current psychotherapy that believes that body and emotions act in concert. It was developed by the late Dr. Frederick S. Perls. One reason why Gestalt can help women especially, is that it builds pride and self-reliance.

Most people waste energy, "Fritz" Perls liked to say in his lectures. He would demonstrate this by making fingerhooks of each hand, then linking his hands together, pulling in opposite directions. "Did you see how much energy I spent doing nothing?" he would ask. "Listening" to your body is important; and learn not to be afraid of your emotions and your senses. We have a life force within us, an *élan vital*. It empowers senses to listen, scout, and describe the world.

Emphasizing that emotions should not be thought of as a nuisance, but as important motors of behavior, Dr. Perls liked to define emotions in the widest sense—as basic energy. This varies in people by what Perls termed hormonic differences. "This basic excitement [is converted by] the adrenal glands, let's say, into anger and fear; by the sex glands into libido." If one is adjusting to a loss, it is turned into grief.

"Every emotion expresses itself in the muscular system," explained Perls. "You can't imagine anger without [showing] muscular movement. You can't imagine joy, which is more or less identical with dancing, without muscular reaction. In grief there is sobbing and crying, and in sex and love there are also certain body movements . . . Any disturbance of this excitement metabolism will diminish your vitality."

Emotions that are not given free expression can congest, then back up and stagnate into anxiety (defined by Perls as a tremendous excitement that is held up, bottled up). At his lectures, at California's Esalen Institute, he dramatized this by narrowing his chest, in gestures to show the way emotions can block the blood vessels, and limit breathing. In inhibited persons, unreleased emotions come to block and desensitize the sensory system: eye strengths deteriorate, ear blocking leads into partial deafness, sexual frigidity grows, and so forth.

Although Perls disagreed with Freud on several levels, he acknowledged Freud's genius in pointing out that many events are *overdetermined*—or have many causes. Accepting this can release many guilts, for some people maintain a tortured responsibility for events and persons they no longer can influence.

Indeed, life today is filled with unfinished *gestalts*, or incomplete situations. Perls liked to quote the ancient Greek philosopher Heraclitus (whose doctrines were so advanced for his day, he was known as Heraclitus the Obscure). It was this pre-Socratic thinker who said, "Nothing is permanent except change." Finding an unexpected relevance for today's fast-moving world, Perls often sprinkled his lectures with another Heraclitus observation—no man steps into the same river twice.*

Perls scorned the use of the word "neurosis," in favor of "growth disorder." Gestalt theory, similarly, emphasizes the concept of the *ego boundary*—an extension of self that does not stop with the individual. It can, and usually does, include husband or lover, children, relatives, friends, club or fraternal association, love of country, and ethnic heritage. Lately, one's job or employer also are being included within one's ego boundary, particularly if one is associated with a benevolent corporation that cultivates loyalty.

But when the ego boundary comes to include possessions and material objects, one makes oneself vulnerable to emotional upheaval at time of their loss or theft. Sometimes such ego identification can be carried too far for emotional health. Re-

---

* Consider this carefully. Are you the same person you were two years ago? (Six months ago?) Perhaps others, too, have grown. Emotional conflicts can be resolved with greater ease when one accepts change in others, as well as oneself.

called Dr. Perls, "In 1929, many people committed suicide because they were so identified with their money that life wasn't worth living any more when they lost it."

The emotionally healthy person keeps her ego boundaries flexible, ready to adapt to changing circumstances. Avoid emotional tenacity, Perls urged. Learn to "let go" of counterproductive situations; stay alert to relationships that require new approaches—or those that cease to exist. The woman who stubbornly fixes her emotional attention onto a situation that no longer rewards or nourishes, becomes her own enemy. "[Such an] overextended contact is as pathological as the complete withdrawal [seen in] the ivory tower, or the catatonic stupor," Perls warned.

Should a person express resentment, or protest a frustrating situation? Yes, indeed.* But speak softly, with words that will not intimidate, if persuasion is your goal. And it fosters mental health to take your emotional nourishment from within, rather than remaining dependent on your environment, social status, or loved ones.

Gestalt says we must learn to depend on our centers,† integrating attention and awareness. We can do this as we become more physical and sensual; this minimizes intellectual rigidities. (Trust your body, Perls liked to say.) He defined responsibility as *response-ability*—the ability to move, free your body excitements and, thereby, release your energetic charge and untapped potential.

Why does the average person live at only 5 to 15 percent of his highest potential? Because we fall into patterned behavior, living in clichés and role-playing. "Some of us play 'Madison Avenue' to convince other people, or ourselves, of our value." We play the same role, over and over again, and thus limit ourselves and our future. "When you learn how you prevent your-

---

* Perls: "Anything unexpressed which wants to be expressed can make you feel uncomfortable."

† Perls used the term "center" to describe what theologians call a "soul"—the feelings and spirit.

self from growing—you have a way of making life richer, making you more and more capable of mobilizing yourself."

The German-born Perls dismissed traditional Freudian psychoanalysis as "mind-fucking." "The great error of psychoanalysis is in assuming that the memory is reality. All the so-called traumata, which are supposed to be the root of the neurosis, are an invention of the patient to save his self-esteem."

It is energy-wasting to lament the past, agree both Gestalt theory and Bioenergetics; this includes any problems of childhood. In a sense, one must learn to "let go" of one's parents. Some people, said Perls, are really collectors of grievances. They do nothing else in their lives but collect grievances and keep them within themselves. ("You can imagine how little vitality they have left for living.")

Dr. Perls deplored the "turn-onners" who merchandise instant sensory awareness, and vaguely identified "therapists" with insufficient training. Encounter groups are faddism, he warned, and as dangerous to workable psychology as the decades-long recline on the analyst's couch. Encounter group "cures" disregard the all-important requirement of self-help—personal growth. They also underestimate the real potential ("the inborn genius") inherent in everybody.

"You have to invest yourself," Fritz would whisper hoarsely, with an open-necked shirt framing his face, wizened, smiling, encouraging. "It takes time to grow."

FIVE WAYS TO RELEASE EMOTIONAL TENSIONS

Experts in these new psychology fields all agree that emotional upset gives birth to tension. To interrupt this self-destructive spiral, here are five self-help techniques. Any one of them may prove appropriate for your needs, the next time you feel knotty from emotional problems. (Again, we note that readers with deep-seated emotional disorders, or chronic tensions, should consult a doctor.)

(1) SHUTTLING: A MENTAL EXERCISE

Fritz Perls developed this technique for persons with occasional anxiety, confusion, or simple boredom. It helps to practice "shuttling" with a friend, or an associate; at the least, use a pad and pencil.

> Sit quietly, body relaxed, and feet flat on the floor. Close your eyes. Let your imagination roam to the most tranquil (or the most pleasant and exciting) incident you remember. If nothing comes to mind, then fantasize. Let your imagination roam free, drawing in the environment, the people, the way they are dressed. Then notice the action that ensues, the interpersonal relationships, the facial expressions of the participants, and their attitudes. Make special note of your own contribution to this moment in time.
>
> Now return to the present. (Make detailed notes.) Compare your present mood with the other situation. (Dr. Perls: "Most likely, the *there* situation was preferable to the *here* situation.") What aspects were different? What persons? Which of your personality traits was emphasized in your reverie? (Record these answers.) Then close your eyes again, and "go away" once more. Again, observe details on the same, or a fresh, situation. Return to the present, and use pad and paper to record all your impressions.

Continue to do this, studying, self-examining, until you find yourself beginning to feel comfortable. If you are lucky, you will then experience a sudden waking up (or a *satori*); this can reveal what may be missing in your present that was responsible for such a feeling of well-being in your memory, or fantasy. This is a "hole," as Perls termed it. It becomes an area for self-improvement, or change. (Perls: "Do this on your own . . . until you come to your senses, and until you begin to see, and hear, and be here in this world; until you really begin to exist.")

(2) THE MIND/EMOTIONAL SPECTRUM
(AN IMAGERY EXERCISE)

Shuttling can unblock frozen perceptions; but there are reverse problems, especially for the sensitive, emotionally active woman. Shakespeare's observation about anger ("Anger is like a full-hot horse, who being allowed his way, self-mettle tires him") says much about the exhausting effect of uncontrolled emotions. Flailing about, such confusion can be ruinous to female vitality. The following imagery exercise is for the woman who needs more self-mastery, rather than the person who requires stimulation. This technique can serve you when you know what is the problem, but, at the same time, sense that you cannot influence the situation. Outside events will advance at their given speed.

> Imagine there is a line connecting your emotions and your intellect. Envision this line as a spectrum, or horizontal gauge. It shades to white on your left, then darkens in hue to deep black on your right. Learn to associate your thoughts with the light-colored, clear side of this mental spectrum—clear judgment, uncolored by emotional bias (cool reason, if you will).
>
> Then let your overview move to the right, as shadings deepen. This end of your spectrum symbolizes inky emotional confusions. Whatever the negative emotion that has intruded itself upon your thinking (hostility, anger, jealousy, suspicion, resentment, outright hatred), it should be labeled as self-destructive. It can destroy vitality, beauty, sound judgment, and—eventually—life itself.
>
> The next time you feel overwhelmed by your emotions, sit back, and envision this mind/emotional spectrum. Breathe deeply, from your lower abdomen. Try to shift your thinking into lighter, cooler subjects. Then distract yourself with a walk around the block, or an absorbing project.
>
> This emotional discipline will not come easy, at first. The concert pianist, or ballerina, requires regular and often monotonous practice to refine her talent. Periodic practice also can improve mind control.

The woman who learns to bring her emotions into check (when they are distorting her judgment) advances considerably in self-esteem. And it has been said, the world belongs to the person who can control his own thoughts.

We are not urging that a woman should maintain an annoying reasonableness. Many emotions—love, pride, joy, and kindness—enrich the daily fabric of our lives. What is important is to learn to reach for these thoughts to replace destructive ones. When your value judgments are based on life's positive emotions, you might not always be right—but you will evolve closer to that noble purpose that obtains life's most bountiful rewards. The Biblical apostle, St. Paul, was delivering sound emotional advice when he suggested: "Whatsoever things are true, whatsoever things are honest, whatsoever things are just, whatsoever things are pure, whatsoever things are of good report . . . Think on these things."

(3) BIOFEEDBACK

One psychiatrist noted that many of life's emotional problems come when a person must cope with sudden loss—of a loved one, a job, money, prestige, a way of life. Adapting to change can be terrifyingly difficult for some. Often it is the most logical woman, who prides herself on "being reasonable," who finds it frustrating to accept life's jolts. (A friend, widowed and rearing four young children, said she learned to live with her bereavement only when she stopped railing at fate, and stopped asking, "Why did this happen to me?")

In my lectures on rejuvenation, I like to point out that all of the world's key religions share a common maxim—the acceptance of things you cannot change. The Hindus call this Karma; Mohammedans say, "Allah wills it." Judeo-Christian belief stresses the Almighty purpose: fate is beyond the power of mortals. Whatever the creed, the leading religions agree that emotional health depends on learning to accept what is inevitable.

Now a Space Age technique, called *biofeedback,** offers a

* If you are unable to locate a biofeedback training center in your city, call the closest university. The psychology department can refer you—or explain ways the public might use the school's biofeedback equipment.

way to help with emotional adaptation. It can provide special help to widows, and others beset with anxieties about the present or future. This method is based on the medical law that the brain gives off various signals, or waves. In a pleasant state of relaxed alertness, the human brain produces a wave called *alpha*. With the aid of special gauges or indicators, a person can monitor her own brain waves, and learn what thoughts affect them. To do this, equipment is used called the electroencephalograph, or EEG.

With biofeedback, learning about yourself becomes amusing, and the results can be astounding. The type of mental imagery that induces relaxation varies, person to person. (I found that images of sunny underwater swims in turquoise Caribbean seas were the most conducive to *alpha*.) What is important is that the biofeedback student learns to reproduce these *alpha* waves, or pleasant relaxation, at will, regardless of surroundings.

Learning emotional control (and adaptation to loss) with biofeedback offers a happy side effect: a woman grows in self-assurance when she learns to summon *alpha* waves at will. And instant relaxation can keep stress from building up, even during an aggravating situation.

(4) EMOTIONAL EXERCISE: TAKE A VACATION
FROM YOUR HANGUP

As we have seen, psychosomatic research has brought sharp insight into the interactions of emotions, mind, and body. Consider the reverse—the phenomenon that occurs when a fatigued body provokes an otherwise logical mind. It brings self-doubts and discord. After a tedious day, you are less capable of steady control than at other times.

Learn to recognize that irritability is a fatigue symptom—and treat it. Remember that when you are tired, you will be less likely to summon enthusiasm for new ideas. Even if your intellectual detachment is noteworthy, you will muster less brain power when physically depleted. The woman who has advanced in self-knowledge learns to postpone any sensitive or testy discussions from late day to mornings. For most persons, mind and body resources have then been recharged.

As an adventure in self-mastery, try to put yourself at emotional distance when a problem looms large. The moment events become really upsetting, try to disengage yourself. Take an emotional vacation. "Tune out" with an escape movie. Or plan a future vacation, or go swimming. Distract yourself for a day, or, better, for several days. Many emotional problems resolve themselves, eventually. Understanding this, you can make time your friend, instead of a bitter (and aging) enemy.

(5) EXERCISE—AS EMOTIONAL RELEASE

Our previous mention of swimming opens up a kind of upsmanship that can reunite body and mind—physical exercise. Leading American exercise specialists (Jack LaLanne, Nick Kounovsky, Manya Kahn) have been saying for years that exertions help women cope with their unique emotionality. Sure, tennis alone won't bring back a wandering husband, or teach a rebellious child to have parental respect. But using physical exertions to relieve tension is a terrific way to restore inner balance. It equips you for coping with your problem, and stressful situations become less unnerving.

Most yoga exercises help to reintegrate body and mind. So can *noncompetitive* recreations like jogging, swimming, fishing, or cycling. Even a brisk walk can brighten your mood. As an extra aid for breaking up emotional stress, open up your mind to the sensory stimulation you encounter along the pathway— the weather, the color of flowers, unusual aromas.

A BODYPOWER RELAXATION TECHNIQUE

The following exercise is a simple meditation. A form of Raja Yoga, it can be practiced anywhere. It is most effective before a tranquil scene, in a garden, or viewing a pleasant painting. (Some mystics use a lighted candle.) If you select a photograph or painting, find one that soothes your emotions, rather than one that excites. Find a single detail to contemplate, for it helps to narrow your field of vision.

Later, you can experiment, with such things as art posters or advertising logo. Anything works that will help you focus inward, reaching for your psychic center. (I have learned to meditate in taxis, and during traffic delays.)

> Focus your gaze on the object or scene. Stare at it fixedly for several seconds, avoiding eye strain. Then close your eyes, and try to sustain the image of the object on the inside of your closed eyelids. Don't be discouraged if the vision disappears; mastery comes with practice. Reopen your eyes and refresh your memory. Now close your eyes and keep them closed. Holding your eyelids lightly shut, mentally continue to re-create the scene until your brain seems filled with it. Do not question, analyze, or turn a quiver of your intellectual machinery. In the fullest possible sense, enjoy existing.
>
> Hold this mental immersion for as long as possible, breathing slowly but regularly, from your abdomen. The longer you can remain "under," the more refreshed you will feel, on your return to your surroundings. Indeed, it requires a few moments to adjust to your outside environment, after deep meditation. This pause for transition is the mark of successful meditation.

Uninterrupted attention to the visual scene is important. It is such single-mindedness that unlocks your tense muscles and releases taut nerves. This exercise is a form of "creative visualization." It is taken from that part of yoga called the "path to Infinite Energy." Practiced regularly, it will lift you toward understanding the truth behind an Oriental concept: *the yogi reaches his goal when the means and the end become the same.*

CHAPTER 15

The Psychophysical Techniques: New Ways to Ease Your Tensions

You can always tell a winner by the confident way she walks. She balances herself with pride while she is speaking. Her neck is relaxed yet lengthened. Her head rides high. Regardless of her weight or body structure, she appears at easy grace with herself—and she radiates this confidence to the rest of her world.

Now there are body awareness techniques that improve mood as well as posture. With them, a woman learns to offset early fatigue by restoring her inner harmonies, or homeostasis. These new techniques are called *psychophysical,* because their developers claim that emotional improvements can result from body work. They are fun to practice; more important, they help a woman understand herself and her sexuality. Such self-knowledge brings renewal—and a uniquely humanitarian form of self-love.

These new methods have various names—the Feldenkrais system, Rolfing, the Alexander Technique. Yet there is a common denominator about all: the student acquires a respect for her body potential that can approach open-mouthed astonishment. At California's Esalen Institute, Will Schutz says: "Chances are that some of the things about your body which you've always considered unchangeable really are: your height, emotional outlook, your self-image, your body proportions." Feldenkrais students have thrown away their glasses. Rolfing claims to restore a tipped uterus. The late F. Matthias Alexander believed that his body coordination method had cosmic significance, in that reintegrating mind and body makes thinking more rational.*

All such practitioners agree that each of their psychophysical techniques will unleash new energy and pride for those who practice them. They all boast different approaches and affect both the body and the personality. They seem to succeed in relieving stress, anxiety, and many of the discomforts felt by women, especially at mid-life. If you feel deeply troubled, talk with a physician or psychotherapist.

THE ALEXANDER TECHNIQUE

One of the earliest pioneers in the psychophysical sciences was F. Matthias Alexander, a nineteenth-century Australian actor who one day lost his voice. The medical advice he received (don't speak and your voice will return) worked only temporarily. Each time he rested, his voice returned to normal, only to be lost again when he went back on the stage.

Obtaining no satisfactory medical explanation for all this, Alexander turned in another direction—into himself. And out of Alexander's preoccupation with his body (especially the interactions of his head, neck, and torso), man's knowledge of physiology took a giant step forward.

EMOTIONS AND THEIR CONSEQUENCES

During Alexander's era (the Victorian period), medical diagnosis was limited. Doctors—as well as the rest of society—

---

* Alexander liked to declare: "I don't care who you bring up, Socrates or anyone else—you will find gaps and holes in his thinking. Let me coordinate him and you will not find gaps and holes in his thinking."

had a disdain, bordering on repugnance, for the living human body. Man's physical being was relegated to a status considered inferior to his soul and the mind (a "cross to be borne," as one historian puts it). A patient being examined by a physician was seated behind a screen. Women were treated with diffidence, when they were treated at all. Any medical research on the body was confined to the dismembering of corpses.

Alexander, however, suspected that the living interactions between various body parts could create stressful tensions. He set up a five-way mirror, and spent nearly ten years studying body interrelationships. He paid special heed to his emotions, and their physical consequences. He noted that most adults come to their maturity, their work, indeed, to all that they do, with posture and body habits acquired unawares, often in childhood. As one Alexander method teacher, Ilana Rubenfeld, describes it, for the first twelve years or so of a person's life, long hours are spent looking up at grownups. ("What this does to the back of the neck can be something gruesome.") Many persons are unconscious of their back rigidities and hunched shoulders. Complicating this, emotional upheaval and personal tragedy can etch psychic memories on our soft, malleable layers of skin. Such tensions make it hard to relax. They must be eased (or unlearned) before gymnastics, ballet, or other body training can take place.

Even in his day, Alexander liked to point out that many supposed advancements of man had a deteriorating effect on the "sense registers" of the body—reflexes that were once used to guide humans in correct use of their bodies. He hated chairs, feeling they symbolized the way that man tends to bring about his own physical deterioration.*

The Alexander Technique uses a unique method to effect postural changes: it teaches each student to find his Tao, or "no-

---

* Biologist Dr. George E. Cognill (an Alexander enthusiast) agreed on this, noting that the chair came very late in our genetic development. "Primitive man sat on the ground, or squatted when not standing . . . This posture requires extreme stretching of the extensor muscles of the legs (when squatting) and abduction of the thighs." Habitual use of the chair, by comparison, restricts this.

place." (Ilana Rubenfeld compares this to the neutral gear on a car.) Once the student has achieved this ability, he has opened up new choices, for he has learned to pause, at midpoint, between a mental command and the body movement that follows it.

While this learning process is under way, the Alexander teacher uses what Rubenfeld terms "laying on of hands." Gently, encouragingly, the instructor tries to manually open up body blocks. This supplies feedback knowledge to help the student "let go." Sometimes painful memories are released.* Ilana Rubenfeld, who trained in Gestalt theory under Dr. Fritz Perls, developed a method that incorporates Gestalt into the Alexander Technique. Now Alexander teachers are being trained in this combined approach, one that was first suggested by Perls himself.

Ilana was practicing and teaching Alexander before it became fashionable, and her case histories attest to the strong link (particularly in women) between the body and the emotions. One client was sent to Ilana by a noted psychoanalyst, to work out physical tensions concurrent with his unsnarling the emotional ones. After weeks of collaboration, the psychotherapist reported real progress. Shortly after this, Ilana was deftly working the woman's shoulders (to broaden chest constrictions and free breathing) when the woman's arms actually seemed to lengthen. Even Ilana had been unaware how rigid she had been holding them. Now, frightened, the woman inexplicably began to cry.

Using Gestalt techniques, Ilana coaxed her client into describing the reason for her tears: she feared some kind of punishment if her arms grew longer! As the woman spoke, her voice tones changed; they became shrill and more juvenile. Asked how old she was, the client (reliving a childhood trauma) whispered, "Two or three; I'm in my crib." Then a new flood of tears released old memories. When calmed, she said she remembered, for the first time since maturity, the colored ribbons with which her mother would tie her tiny hands to her crib—a punishment to prevent her from masturbating.

---

* Some patients are afraid to let go of certain body parts, according to various Alexander teachers I interviewed.

BODY AWARENESS EXPERIMENT

The typical Alexander student of today is a person with minor emotional problems, and major body tensions. For anyone curious to glimpse her own body awareness possibilities, Ilana suggests the following experiment.

> Close your eyes, relaxing completely. Now focus your mind's attention on your right thumb. Pause; eyes still closed, move your attention down to your right foot, gently and gradually. Focus on the third toe in your right foot. (Remove your shoes if you like: Do whatever you need to do to sense your third toe as a separate body part.) Maintain this sensation for several moments. Then, slowly, open your eyes.

Did you take off your shoes and touch your toe? Did you wiggle your toe? Whatever you did, you gradually began to form what is termed a *kinesthetic awareness* of your body parts. With practice, this can improve your neural network; it can blaze a new pathway in your brain. This will enhance and enrich your awareness of your entire body.

The Alexander Technique has surprising relevancy in today's world, where stress can immobilize anyone. Because it emphasizes body regions where tensions seem to originate (especially below the head and the neck), the Alexander Technique can even offset the effects of noise pollution!*

---

* In recent years there have been "startle pattern" tests at Tufts University, that confirmed the Alexander Technique. Using multiple-channel electromyography, Dr. Frank Pierce Jones measured human reflex responses from a range of noises: the slamming of doors, dropped objects, a revolver shot. Reported Dr. Jones: in all cases where the noise was strong enough to bring a response, it appeared in the neck muscles. In some cases, the response appeared nowhere else. For most persons, such neck tensions brought on tensions elsewhere in the body.

ROLFING, OR STRUCTURAL INTEGRATION

At polar opposites from the logic of the Alexander Technique is the work of Ida Rolf—who developed Structural Integration. This method is couched in technical jargon, and consists almost exclusively of manipulative massage. It is sometimes painful, and is bold in its claims of psychiatric and gynecological cures.

Structural Integration differs from the other major psychophysical methods in that it emphasizes the importance of gravity —and the body's relationship to it. Dr. Ida P. Rolf has dedicated her career to the belief that stress and emotional problems are eased once the body is brought into a balanced relationship with the field of gravity. Her work is termed Rolfing by her followers.

Structural Integration is based on the theory (not found in medical textbooks) that there are three layers, or "bags," within the body; Rolf calls them *fascia*. These "three bags that hold one together"—as one Rolfer terms it—are variously named superficial, superficial deep, and deep fascia. To explain the need for fascia support, Ida Rolf uses a tent-pole simile. When soft body tissue is appropriately positioned, in relation to gravity, the body is held with minimal effort. Otherwise a constant state of biological alert exists.

Dr. Rolf, in chatting with me, repeatedly used the term "random body" to describe those physiques most in need of Rolfing and gravity readjustments. "The ordered body is supported by gravity." In all cases, she added, "Gravity is the therapist."

Her U.S. practitioners number about 125 at this writing. They don't feel the same cautions that Ida Rolf does about promising what Structural Integration can, and cannot, do—and this seems to annoy Dr. Rolf. When I told her that one prominent Rolfer claims that Structural Integration can cure complex forms of mental illness, she muttered, almost to herself, "We have got to keep out of our vocabulary certain words that belong in the medical field—such as the word, 'cure.' "

Rolfers also claim that their rigorous massage will relieve menstrual cramps and certain sexual disorders. A range of female disorders can result from a displaced pelvis, according to Ida Rolf. When the female pelvis is misaligned, she claims, everything inside that region will be under stress.

Can Structural Integration reverse a tipped uterus? Dr. Rolf did not hesitate after my question. "Very definitely," she stated. Pressed as to whether before-and-after proof exists to medically document such claims, she shrugged aside the idea. "We don't go in for medical things."

Partial documentation for Rolfing has come from Dr. Julian Silverman who devised an ingenious battery of tests to verify body changes after Structural Integration treatments. Dr. Silverman (now director of Esalen Institute) declined my request for a comparison of Rolfing with the benefits of traditional psychoanalysis. But in his 1973 report, "Stress, Stimulus Intensity Control and the Structural Integration Technique," he described various tests that showed body-mind improvements from Rolfing. These tests included biochemical measurements, eye movement procedures, personality evaluations, and other psychophysical criteria.

Psychologists, neurophysiologists, patients, and mere bystanders all seem to agree that Rolfing changes things. Whether this is due to gravity* and the body's relationship to it is not clear. In linking technical physics to the physical, Ida Rolf may be on shaky ground. I asked Texas cardiologist Dr. Lawrence Lamb, affiliated with the N.A.S.A. astronaut program, whether gravity was an aging influence. Not really, he replied, adding that a total absence of gravity (as in the state of weightlessness) in itself can be unhealthy. From birth, human beings learn adaptation to gravity as we know it on this planet. Once this force is upset, or interfered with, an unnatural condition results.

Is *fascia*, or connective tissue (as it is medically termed), really so important? In itself, is this really a cause of stress? As medical evidence for her theories, Dr. Rolf cites the work of Canada's Dr. Hans Selye. Being familiar with Selye's work and

---

* One of Ida Rolf's followers claims that Rolf uses "gravity" in the sense of the German word, "*schwergewicht*," or "body weight."

his writings, I asked Ida Rolf where—in any of his works—did he emphasize a direct relationship between connective tissue and biological stress? All through his books, she snapped. Yet my research has failed to unearth any such documentation. His major work, which I mentioned to Rolf, *The Stress of Life*, gives just a passing reference to connective tissue. (It is mentioned only for its role in arthritis and the inflammation phenomenon.) As we have seen, more specific causes are shown to trigger the stress-response: drugs, emotional depression, cold. For the stress syndrome is essentially an overreacting of *internal* body systems, such as the endocrines and the thymus-lymph glands.

But just as F. Matthias Alexander was considered a charlatan by some and a genius by others, so Ida Rolf might have stumbled onto a space age technique that is peculiarly appropriate to our disruptive times. At 79, feisty Ida Rolf works 12 to 15 hours daily and she credits Structural Integration with her stamina. The most costly* of the psychophysical techniques, a typical ten-hour Rolfing course costs from $300 to $400, depending on where you reside.

Using the language of this brave new world, Will Schutz, a former California Rolfer, tells in his memoirs of his experiences. He found that "the backs of the legs are very alien, difficult places to have much feeling." Such a body region shows tensions from "holding back"—for the legs bear the brunt of presenting a relaxed, stable image to the rest of the world. "Control issues," also, somehow relate to the backs of the legs, primarily as a "resistance to control" by others. At the same time, a repressed desire to control others can be revealed by tensions in those body muscles that bend the joints: the flexors. Tension in the back can relate to "digging in your heels," or stiffening the backbone. These are examples of literal body blocks and postures of habitual resistance.

Schutz tells of a patient whose Rolfing reaction brought her

---

* There are reports of students who have discontinued Rolfing (because it was painful) and others who migrated to the Alexander Technique after traumatic Rolfing experiences.

into emotional contact with an early sexual experience. A virgin at 13, she agreed to be the sexual subject for an older man. "When the sex became painful (my partner was trying anal penetration), I resisted, complained, and asked for the act to cease. My partner was too far into his own trip to care," she recalls. "So I had to endure until he climaxed." After additional Rolfing, the girl appeared able to discuss the incident calmly. Once the memory was fully exposed, she felt "a great sense of relief."

Dr. John C. Lilly tells of a similar Rolfing experience, in his autobiography. Lilly's early work (teaching dolphins to talk, isolation studies in Caribbean seclusion tanks, and sensory-deprivation research) gave him scientific credentials which made him worthy of treatment by Ida Rolf personally. She seemed to have the ability to scan his body and quickly zero in on those areas of deepest tension. During a later massage session, another Rolfer came across a faded foot scar. Lilly, as a young bush cutter in Oregon, had acquired it in an accident, years earlier. His ax had slipped, going deep into his foot. On seeing blood spurting up from beneath the underbrush, his first reaction was that he had accidently cut the little dog that belonged to the foreman of the work crew. Then, decades later, as a Rolfer touched that almost-forgotten scar, an airplane came within earshot. There was "fantastic energy release," says Lilly, as the jet hum simultaneously went through his senses, recalling for him the trauma of pain. "During this, I saw the ax descending over my foot, and very slowly cutting the skin, the first layer of subcutaneous tissue, the fascia, the ligaments, and going down into the bone."

But this time he felt the pain of the entry of the ax into his skin which somehow he had missed in the original happening. "Suddenly I realized that I had blocked the pain in the original experience."* Until the day he was Rolfed, Lilly had not put

* Lilly adds, "This scar . . . had a basic traumatic memory, a [subconscious] tape loop attached to it."

equal weight on that particular foot as he walked. As he describes it, he had created a "hole" in his body image. "The Rolfing allowed this hole to fill in, allowed my posture to improve in respect to that foot, and the realization of the pain passed away."*

Dr. Lilly was twice fortunate: his memory was a physical pain, rather than a trauma with deep emotional roots. So his Rolfer could cope with his reactions. But what of the emotional trauma that (according to psychophysical theory) might be locked beneath the skin surface? Critics of Rolfing point out that Rolfers are not psychologists, nor trained to deal with emotional trauma if it should arise. And even Rolfers agree that body work can release forgotten emotional memories.

What type of woman would benefit most from Rolfing? If you're just a little lazy, sensuous, nervous, and, perhaps, a bit overweight, Rolfing might be just right for you. The woman who prefers to follow a diet doctor's shortcuts rather than count calories for herself (like the woman who'll seek out an astrologer rather than chart her own horoscope) might find a genuine esthetic pleasure in being Rolfed. Rolfing does not always bring pain—but it can for some.

Ultimately, as Ida Rolf warns, the real basis of Structural Integration is a way of approaching life, a new way of thinking. Despite the fact that it is intimately physical, Rolfing requires considerable mental discipline for lasting results.

BUILDING TOWARD PERFECTIBILITY: THE FELDENKRAIS EXERCISES

Dr. Moshe Feldenkrais is the man who has brought twenty-first-century attitudes and concepts to the psychophysical sci-

* From the Lilly autobiography, *The Center of the Cyclone*, The Julian Press, 1972.

ences. A leading industrial designer before his interest in yoga and the Alexander Technique propelled his genius down new psychophysical paths, Dr. Feldenkrais brings an engineering approach to body studies; this provides a revolutionary insight into the human machine. Today, leading neurologists, psychologists and doctors specializing in rehabilitative medicine travel to his sunny studio in Israel to study with the man whom David Ben-Gurion credited with rejuvenating his body and his spirit at the age of 70.

Feldenkrais believes that man, or woman, can self-evolve and reach a higher perfectibility—not by suppressing animal instincts, but by building upon them, and by learning to guide one's physical reins with body awareness. As with other followers of Wilhelm Reich, Feldenkrais sees many emotions as physical by-products.

For example, many persons add body weight first in the buttocks area. Reich claimed that this is a form of body armor, put up by the being to insulate certain body parts from interpersonal contact. (In the case of women who avoid sexual relationships—and grow fatty layers about the hips—this combination of symptoms is known as the "frozen pelvis syndrome.")

The Feldenkrais system of exercises offers extra rewards for women, those over thirty especially, due to the way it can retard aging. Certain biologists point to the fact that the body has various aging timetables, with some parts aging faster than others. This is explained by a cellular theory: There are two kinds of body cells, those that can reproduce themselves, and those that cannot. In the first category are our blood, skin, and liver cells. Nerve and brain cells are in the second group—they cannot replicate. Once these latter cells begin to die off, a downhill descent into aging and deterioration begins. (In this regard, it is not surprising that loss of memory—requiring brain cells— is one of the first signs of advancing age.) For many women, neural dysfunction, or deterioration of the nervous system, comes early. And the more emotional (and sensitive) a woman is —the more likely she is to have prematurely aged her nervous system. This is especially true of women who live in big cities, or crowded households.* Yet Feldenkrais says, whatever your sex, age, or lifestyle, you can learn to tap *dormant* areas of the brain (this might be the left or right hemisphere; a lot depends upon whether you are habitually right- or left-handed). Then you come to revitalize your entire nervous system.

Employ your body parts in unaccustomed ways, suggests Feldenkrais. Wear your wristwatch on your other arm. Play an occasional game of left-handed tennis or Ping-Pong. Give your brain new options—it will automatically select the most efficient way to do things. This also will conserve energy, for, as Feldenkrais says: It is easier to play correctly on an instrument that is in tune than on one that is not.

Even the most fit person may be unwittingly misusing her body. Would you like to learn more about your own reactions? Perform this simple experiment.

> Stand upright, legs a comfortable distance apart, torso relaxed. Extend your arms forward at waist level. Pretend you are holding a really heavy bag of cement, weighing about 150 pounds. Really consider this weight, and attempt to lift it. Lift high, higher. Try to imagine the pressure of all this, pushing down on your arms and outstretched hands.

Now think back to the beginning of this test. Chances are that you stopped breathing when you began to "lift" the imaginary weight. Or, preparing for the chore, you took a deep breath as you began. According to Feldenkrais, both of these practices are wrong; they subject the body to stress and unneeded tension. This jumbles muscular coordination. It forces your muscles to work against the commands from your brain, rather than in easy unison. (Next time, exhale as you lift!)

You can learn to convert such energy conflicts into easy body interaction with the Feldenkrais system, making less motion accomplish more.

---

* Today one hears big city teen-aged girls saying, "I'm too nervous to do that." Or, "Staying around him (or her, or it) makes me nervous." Before 1950, such plaints were more likely to come from the lips of the elderly.

The new sensory-physical victories that body awareness brings will be most appreciated by women; for often we might have felt limited, or victimized, by our frailties, and tensed up by environmental forces outside our control. And, due to its message in rehabilitative medicine, this method offers new vistas for the injured, the crippled, the arthritic, and infirm and older persons. Yet mastering this unusual exercise system is not easy. In these pages, we can provide just a sampling of what an intensive Feldenkrais instruction session, one-to-one with a trained instructor, would be like. Try this curious exercise:

> Standing, eyes closed, extend your arms forward at shoulder level. Now imagine a ray of light, traveling from the index finger of your right hand to your left eye. Eyes still closed, maintain this image as you envision another light ray, this one traveling from your left index finger to your right eye. Try to mentally feel the point where the two light rays seem to cross. Take your right thumb and your index finger and mark that point in space, eyes still closed.

When you open your eyes to look, it is unlikely that the place that you chose will be correct. Furthermore, says Feldenkrais, if you repeat the experiment, using the thumb and the index finger of your left hand, a different location will be selected!

YOU AND YOUR SELF-IMAGE

A person's self-image can become unknowingly distorted over the years. Feldenkrais claims that physical self-image and true reality may be as much as 300 percent apart, even for the emotionally stable and the physically fit.

Yet your psychic ideas about yourself influence the way you hold your chest, the way you position your shoulders and head, and your voice. They determine the way you project your personality and your contacts with others. When your thoughts are negative, defeatist, or depressed, your body reveals this. And,

Feldenkrais says, the reverse is true, also: When your body is held confidently, *your mood lightens.* Many persons, he says, base their self-images on the way they are valued by society. Unfortunately, what results can be emotional and postural chaos. "Like a man trying to force a square peg into a round hole," so the individual strains to fit into the hole that he most wants to fill. Failing in this, his self-value can become so weakened it discourages any further effort. For most persons, less than ten percent of the potential nervous system is used in daily life. A favorite Feldenkrais experiment will demonstrate this.

Standing, extend your right hand to the side of you, at shoulder level. Keeping your eyes on your fingertips, turn your entire torso to the right as far as possible without strain. Then return to forward position, after marking with your eyes how far you turned. Repeat this. Now turn your head to the *left* as you twist your body to the right. This might feel awkward, but do it anyway. (Will Shutz says, "Be very alert to the fact that you have never done this before. In Feldenkrais exercise, awareness is crucial.") Then repeat this head-left and body-right turning, again remarking on the newness of this movement. Perform this five times, until it seems to flow in harmonious grace. Now turn eyes and body *left* and head *right.*
Then repeat your original turn, moving torso, head, and eyes, all turning right at the same time. You will notice how much farther, now, you can turn.

What has happened is that you have provided your neural brain with new options. This permitted your brain to choose the better motor-neural coordination. It expanded your aptitudes and ability.

There are over 1,400 Feldenkrais exercises, at this writing: one key to all of them is that the student never forces her body. There are times when a strength-of-purpose can prove self-defeating, for the body will end up performing a muscular action and its opposite, simultaneously. "Will power may tend to cover up an inability to carry out the action properly," Feldenkrais says. "The right way is to learn to eliminate the efforts opposing the goal, and to employ will power (or force) only when a *superhuman* effort is required."

Feldenkrais exercises are seemingly simple, but some require as many as 25 repetitions for success. The object is to feed new information into the brain's computer—providing options for body efficiency.

Feldenkrais imagery exercises, on the other hand, require little or no movement. Based on advanced yoga, these thought exercises are reminiscent of Indian mystics who learn to, at will, flood any part of their body with extra blood—or selectively lower their own blood pressure. (Knowledge of this inspired scientists at Rockefeller University. They taught mice to "blush" in a certain ear, an accomplishment that eventually led to today's biofeedback studies and equipment.)

It is helpful to run through a physical exertion mentally before doing it, says Feldenkrais, the way musicians soundlessly run through a score before a performance. (Says Esalen Institute's Will Schutz: "I play better handball, now that I do an imaginary run-through prior to game time. My mental warmup frees locked muscles.") *

My favorite Feldenkrais exercise is an imaginary "body painting." Practiced regularly, it is revitalizing and brings a toning effect to body parts. Choosing a suitable time and occasion (at least 40 minutes after mealtime), try this "body painting" experiment for yourself.

> Lie back, breathing deeply, eyes closed. Try to concentrate on reducing all muscular tension, head to toes. Take several minutes if necessary. Then pick a color of paint (bright pink, perhaps, for vivid imagery). With an imaginary brush held over your prone body, begin at your head, and symbolically paint each surface area. Slowly move your mind along your

---

* American football star Jim Brown agrees. He will rehearse every possible play of a key game in his head—in advance. Olympics champion Bill Toomy also engages in mental practice sessions. Sitting still, he imagines the "feel" of every body movement for pole vaulting. He claims this has improved his vaulting ability, as much as athletic practice.

body, carefully and deliberately. (This exercise should take at least four minutes.) Take time to go inside your ears, under your nostrils. Go back around the curve of your neck, and between your shoulders. Gently move down and around your entire torso. Whisk the imaginary paint brush inside the curve of your buttocks, and across the vaginal area. Then move it down and around each leg, slowly. Paint each toe, separately, and slowly.

Now lie back and recall your experience. Were there any body parts that you had difficulty in painting? (The coccyx, ears, the small of your back, the arches of your feet?) Any body part that you do not feel "in touch with" is an area in which aches, psychosomatic tension, and even microbes can settle, according to Feldenkrais.

Most Americans are least "in touch" with their backs. Many women find difficulty painting their buttocks and pelvic areas. For others, the neck is most vulnerable. (This is one reason why there are more sore throats today, says Schutz.) If injuries would be likely in such body regions, the reverse might be possible. With practice, imagery exercises might shore up and strengthen weak cellular groups. At one Feldenkrais demonstration, a student asked balding Will Schutz whether he thought Feldenkrais techniques could avoid hair loss. "If I knew years ago what I know now," said Schutz, "I could have 'gone inside' the hair follicles, one by one. Baldness is a choice."

Many Feldenkrais students have overcome needs for glasses. This is not for everybody—yet the futuristic Israeli scientist says that we "choose" to be far-sighted or near-sighted. Try this eye exercise for yourself.

Imagine that your right eyeball is going up while your left eyeball goes down. Hold this for five seconds, then reverse. Relax your eyes briefly, then repeat this. Practice daily for improved vision.

The Feldenkrais system, like the Alexander Technique, forces the student to find his "tao," or "no-place" (the time just after your brain issues a command, before your muscular system acts on it). Feldenkrais emphasizes the value of the exhaled breath. He cites as an example the shout used by students of the Oriental martial arts (such as karate and kung fu); they employ it at the moment of attack. The advantage is physical, as well as psychological: the forceful shout coordinates all muscular forces for striking, lifting, or pushing. The next time you pick up a heavy bag of groceries (or push open a heavy door), exhale as you move.

CHAPTER 16

Psychophysical
Do's and Don'ts

I hope by now you have experienced some of the possibilities of Bodypower through the exercises and techniques discussed in the foregoing chapters. This is only a beginning, and meant as a guide to the vast possibilities a truly awakened body and mind can bring to you. While we have been concentrating on ways to free the body, all freedoms depend finally on rules. There are certain guidelines that can enlighten and enlarge our experience, rather than restrict it, and I have listed a few below. Think about them—and *enjoy* the results!

DON'T undertake any of the psychophysical therapy suggested in the preceding chapters without a medical checkup. In addition to the benefits of a doctor's opinion, a medical endorsement will increase the likelihood of deducting such treatments on major medical insurance plans as physical therapy.

DO discuss finances before signing any agreements. At this writing, Rolfing costs from thirty to forty U.S. dollars an hour; the Alexander Technique from fifteen to twenty an hour. Feldenkrais is still so new that qualified instructors charge whatever the local traffic will support.

DON'T try Rolfing, if you're pain-sensitive. The group shuns comparison with osteopathy; however I have seen agonizing (albeit brief) pain spasms from those whose bodies required realignment by forceful pressure. At the same time, some who have experienced Rolfing say it has changed their lives—for the better.

DO give the Alexander Technique a try if you'd find a lifelong study you can continue on your own. (One cannot "Rolf" alone.)

DON'T dismiss these new methods as massage or mere posture lessons. I have seen documented before-and-after photos of physical improvements—and these patients boasted personality changes, as well.

DO ask to see professional credentials before you trust your body and your emotions to unqualified hands. Most practitioners of the methods described in this chapter must have at least two years' college education, prior to starting psychophysical training.

DON'T confuse psychophysical therapy with the benefits of a weight loss diet. However, when dieting is hopeless, the body looks slimmer after tension knots are released and correct posture can make you look taller. (New York Alexander teacher Inez Zeller says Alexander can bestow a smaller waistline.)

DO take chronic anxieties or deep depressions to a medically trained psychotherapist. Bioenergetics experts are trained to cope with such emotional disorders. Bioenergetics therapy might take longer, but you'll unveil a super personality—along with your revitalized body.

DON'T discuss the joy you discover in your psychophysical contacts. In yoga, we say that too much verbalizing about sensation will dilute the impact. (As one Alexander teacher warns: Don't "talk away" the experience.)

DO expect miracles, perhaps minor, perhaps astounding. Even the person content with her age and looks will feel a brand-newness after Alexander, Rolfing, or the insights of Feldenkrais. Sleep comes more readily. Sudden noises are less jarring. Stress is less noticeable. You'll be more tolerant of people. You'll find you take better care of yourself, avoiding any deteriorations that could diminish your new body song.

CHAPTER 17

How Top Achievers Cope

My years of interviewing the leaders of various professions, including theatrical celebrities, have shown ways that, to paraphrase F. Scott Fitzgerald, the elite differ from the rest of us. For one thing, those who gain fame from their own pluck, luck, and talent learn to risk themselves regularly. They are not afraid of first-time challenges. This contributes to growth, for—through outreach—they come to use a larger percentage of their inner resources and talents.

A stamina boost seems to come with success, itself, even success on minor levels. As we shall discuss later in this chapter, public recognition (and the self-esteem that this builds) works to ignite a fresh energy supply. We'll term this the "plus ultra factor."

More than ordinary people, achievers acquire an overview of their day-to-day lives. If they dissipate one night, they'll pamper their bodies afterward, sometimes spending days revitalizing. Thus they learn to pace their energies, and try to get the most out of each passing week. (This self-management is probably true among your own community leaders, also. There is a saying in civic work: "When you want the best chairman for your fundraising campaign, find the busiest person in town!")

Some talented people seem to burn themselves out early, for various reasons (*Marilyn Monroe, Janis Joplin, James Dean*). But persons who are steady successes, year after year, learn to blend and perfect a personal recipe for fitness. And since a youthful figure and good looks mean money in the bank, many theatrical stars also concoct their own recipes for weight control.

Joan Crawford told me that, like most long-time film stars, she learned to make weight-watching a *daily* habit. She attributes her energy and a figure that is trim-waisted at 67 years to the fact that she never eats bread, butter, or potatoes. *Marlene Dietrich*, although slightly deaf, is remarkably clear-eyed and smooth of skin and demeanor at 74 years. She was an advocate of organic foods long before nutrition for beauty became fashionable. In Hollywood, during the forties, she often gave gift packets of natural vitamins or soy nuts to co-workers. *Gloria Swanson*, also, is convinced that foods with chemical additives are aging. Even when dining out, she carries her own food with her. She also avoids the company of people who, in one way or another, are unstimulating to be around.

David Niven attributes his perpetual trimness to the fact that he avoids "nonsense foods," such as pretzels, potato chips and hors d'oeuvres.* *Charlton Heston* is a frequenter of the world's great restaurants. Yet at all times he declines difficult-to-digest foods and eats lightly. He prefers lean steaks, particularly when readying himself for a strenuous movie role. He is a daily jogger. *Kitty Carlisle* maintains that ageless chic of hers by watching her diet constantly and retreating annually to a health spa. She says her energies are largely due to her habit of snatching a daily afternoon nap, religiously and without interruption. (It's psychologically helpful, she suggests, to get undressed for such midday rest.)

Ann Miller keeps her dancing energy high with bi-weekly rehearsal hall workouts, and she diets with the show business "dancer's diet." Not recommended for everybody, this high

---

* The French never conceived of such savories as energy fare. The name "hors d'oeuvres" comes from a term meaning "outside of work."

protein crash diet consists of a hard-boiled egg, three times a day, plus lots of water and exercise.*

THE WINNING PERSONALITY

Inside or outside of show business, a pleasant personality is key to showcasing one's talents. Confidence helps, certainly. And there are other attitudes and ego strengths one can cultivate to speed one along the circuitous road to success. *Barbara Walters,* America's most televised hostess-performer, learned an executive success secret at her alma mater, Sarah Lawrence College. Useful in every role of life, the theory consists of figuring out what the next place is in the world that you want most—then beginning to act as if it is yours already. If there's a job vacancy (or a prospective husband!) that you wish, and for which you feel qualified, then conduct your daily life as if your goal is yours already. Dress for it, groom for it, gear your personality to such a life change. This be-what-you-would-be-next formula has worked in a surprising number of cases. When management looks around for the next boss (or your beau gets ready for marriage), the most obvious choice is before their eyes, ready and poised. This is putting an idea of Thoreau's into practice; he defined this strategy when he suggested: "If one advances confidently in the direction of his dreams, and endeavors *to live the life which he has imagined,* he will meet with a success unexpected in common hours."

Elizabeth Ashley is an actress who agrees that a woman, especially, must work out her own prescriptions for living, rather than using those of the rest of the world. Brought up in the traditions of the Old South, she feels that too many women are encouraged to repress their true feelings. What happens is that we stuff our unpleasant reactions and feelings into a gunnysack, which "gets bigger and bigger and finally explodes."

The winning attitude can be as important as talent in making

---

* Like any other unbalanced nutrition, this diet should not be continued for longer than a few days.

your life a success, according to perennial achiever *Lucille Ball*. It helps to enjoy the small successes, thereby building a day-to-day optimism, she suggests. "Don't let the brightness of that big goal blind you to what happens on the way toward the goal. Meet one wave at a time." Gloom and pessimism, she adds, are undertows to be painstakingly avoided.

Serenity is important in a life of activity. But often those minds that are mentally agile have most difficulty obtaining it. One who combined both attributes was *Helena Rubinstein*, the late cosmetics pioneer. An example of the way an active mind keeps a body vigorous decades longer than most, she was reportedly 93 when she died; her family suspects she was much older. Her favorite stress-release was conspicuously displayed in all her homes, from Paris to Park Avenue—fine paintings. Visiting her Manhattan triplex, I noticed that she had special chairs, designed and placed for quiet contemplation before her beloved Dali paintings.

ENERGY THROUGH WORK

One curious factor that seems to hasten success in life is: responsibility. In a survey of the lives of 14,622 achievers throughout history, one American psychologist found that responsibility galvanizes people into taking action, and making a fuller use of their natural capabilities. Even when it means taking on stupendous burdens, being totally involved eventually can lighten your life.

This maxim of responsibility-reinforces-motivation has a side effect that is part of our success theme: developing good financial sense. Money worries can prove such a stressor that two experts cited financial insecurity as a major cause of stress in a recent report. Achievers like *Bob Hope, Bing Crosby, Lucille Ball, Jack Haley*, the late *Jack Benny*, and such social world leaders as *Mary Lasker* and banking wizard *Mary Roebling* learned to save during their peak earning period. This absolved them of later frustrations, freeing their minds and permitting more relaxing pursuits than a sweaty chase after that elusive goddess, financial success.

Of course, money for money's sake becomes its own stressor; (and as Montaigne, the eighteenth-century French philosopher, observed, for some, fame and tranquility can never be bedfellows). Today there are jobs that bring rewards other than financial ones. Dr. Hans Selye terms such activity the play-professions. Discovering the job that is appropriate for one's unique talents and personal needs might take decades. But, once realized, such work becomes self-renewing for the worker.

In this regard, making one's living at the work one most enjoys could explain the energy secret of show business personalities. They became successful in professions that, in most cases, they entered for the fun of it.

Selye points out that joy in one's work contributes to health and longevity, especially if your labors are recognized and applauded. "The most eminent among the hard workers in almost any field became very old," he notes. "Think of *Leonardo da Vinci, Pablo Casals, Henry Ford, Bertrand Russell.*" Even the lesser-known (and often under-salaried) Nobel scientists bear out this concept: *Otto Loewi, Szent-Gyorgyi, Waksman, Rous, Warburg.* "All these men continued to be successful—and what is more important, on the whole, happy—well into their seventies, eighties, or even nineties."[*]

Perhaps finding deep satisfaction in one's work doubles your interest in doing it well. For a zeal for excellence opens up untapped channels within oneself—insists Selye. "You must really want to win to be totally mobilized for a fight. That is why great peaks of accomplishment were achieved by the gladiators and toreadors who had to fight or die, by the saints who gladly endured torture and even death to please God—and by the patriots who considered it an honor to die for king or country."

Certain of the top achievers surveyed have had serial mar-

---

[*] Having interviewed the great and near-great since 1950, I'll add my own observation. Almost to a man, the front runners in the world's prominent professions share another trait: the ability to laugh during trying times.

riages; a few never married. Some have been fortunate enough
to work out a lifelong partnership with a mate that nurtures
and encourages. But one fact stands out in all cases: leading
professionals seem to avoid bad marital relationships. They
leave the marriage that turns sour. Stress expert Walter McQuade
points out that emotional turbulence in an unhappy marriage is
an energy depleter. Boredom is another factor that can hold you
back. When a person settles into a routine of least resistance, it
ages one prematurely.

After widowhood or divorce, many traditionalist women found
they had professional training they did not know they possessed,
for domestic talents can now be commercialized into dollars.
Many real estate agents, caterers, wedding consultants, baking
tycoons, and runaway home-product successes (such as America's
Dilly Beans, started by two Washington, D.C., women), began
small, then gained momentum by grit, adventurousness, and
timing.

Selye likes to point out that only death brings an absence of
stress. By and large, actors and entertainers learn to handle stress
with more dexterity than most people. Perhaps this is because
their moments of greatest stress are also their moments of psychic
fulfillment: applause balances the agonies it costs to obtain it.
This relates, as well, to a curious energy boon that entertainers
and athletes share—a "second wind," usually when they most
need it.

THE PHENOMENON OF THE "SECOND WIND"

For a publication of the American Medical Association,
comedian *Bob Hope* pointed to this concept, claiming it explained
his abundant energies on worldwide army base tours. "We all
have more energy than we realize or use," he noted.

"Most people who have participated in the more strenuous
sports have experienced the phenomenon known as 'second wind.'

When we reach what seems to be the absolute end of our physical endurance, we somehow suddenly achieve an amazing fresh charge of energy—or second wind—which enables us not only to continue but to increase our pace."

At age 73, he recalled there were times in his life when he was exhausted to the point of collapse, even before a performance. Yet his fatigue seemed to vanish when the overture music started up, and he knew there was an audience, out there, that had come to see him. "Suddenly, I have enough adrenaline flowing to run Grand Coulee Dam."

Usually, it's those entertainers who have kept their weight trim who note such a physical response. For years, on musty tours of vaudeville houses, *Bob Hope* formed the habit of seeking out local tearooms in each town. Those were the restaurants likely to serve tiny portions; there he was not tempted to gorge or imbibe alcohol excessively. For, like the majority of smooth-faced, ageless stars, he doesn't smoke, and favors nonalcoholic beverages.

The longer a top performer has been a success, the more likely she or he is to respect enlightenment, thinking it a sign of true achievement. The late actor-producer *Larry Blyden* took brave and curious turns on his road to enlightenment. He told Pat Collins, of CBS-TV, about seeking out a noted guru in Kashmir, in northern India. "He was sitting quietly, meditating, when I first saw him. He appeared to be surrounded by a pool of light." When asked for a simple way to begin a search for psychic energy, the guru suggested the following: "Pause briefly, three times a day. Then consider the fact that you are breathing. Don't do anything about it, at first. Simply recognize that there is a miracle of respiration that exists within you."*

In complex ways, turning in one's psyche to universal human goodness, will build one's own self-esteem. And, more than anything else, this celebration of self is central to the super-energy of top achievers. It can be learned by anybody: From the person

---

* An effortless, gradual way to build body awareness, this technique can prove useful to problem dieters. Indeed, it will deepen motivation for anybody's health or beauty regimen.

who makes herself the best cake-baker on the block, to the fastest stenotypist in the law office, each learns to use more of herself and her innate talent—to relish the thrill that comes from being *numero uno* in some regard. Minor victory can gratify the doer as much as heroic efforts—and spur you forward to adventure and challenge.

Feminist-actress *Marlo Thomas* reminds us that, once a woman begins to feel really good about herself, everything she does will be better, richer, fuller. With heightened confidence, this self-renewal that comes to achievers can keep you zestful in spirit and ready to push off for new horizons.

An exciting, innovative, challenging century awaits us, just around the corner. Times have never been better for women, for the mature woman especially. Women are learning to make new assessments of themselves; of their bodies, their minds and their goals. The world has finally opened up to women, and women may be the most surprised to discover what miraculous creatures they are. Nowhere is this clearer than in the untapped potentials of the human body. Once a woman learns to know, and to love, her body, it will never disappoint her. As you enjoy the full power of it, you will become the full person you were meant to be. And then, like poet Walt Whitman, you too will "sing the body electric."

CHAPTER 18

Self-Realization

Behavioral scientists tell us that self-defeating or negative thought patterns can condition a person for future failure. Yet, whatever your age or background, you can superimpose winning mental patterns upon self-limiting ones. To learn more about your personal mystiques, answer "yes" or "no" to the following questions:

(1) In the past month, have you lied or somehow misrepresented the truth about yourself or about a situation?

(2) If you are married, do you continue to use your husband's name socially and professionally? (Mrs. John Smith, instead of Mrs. Betty Smith.)

(3) Are you hesitant to bring up unpleasant topics for fear your boss or loved ones won't approve?

(4) Do you have relatives or friends with whom you avoid speaking, due to an ancient disagreement?

(5) Do you like to remind yourself of the adjustment problems you endured after recent life changes? (Moving to a new address, a divorce, and so forth.)

(6) Have you let six months go by without seeking out new friends at church or civic group?

(7) Do you spend as much time speaking of the events, and people, of yesterday as making plans for tomorrow?

(8) Do you like to carefully analyze acquaintances?

(9) Are you reluctant to express hostility or anger?

(10) In the past three months, have you declined a new job (or civic or club office) because it calls on you to do things you aren't accustomed to doing?

(11) Do you notice that, lately, life seems empty?

(12) Does the thought of failure seem to hold you back from trying new things?

Each of the foregoing will be answered "no" by the woman who is still evolving and growing as a person. Otherwise, there is no scoring for this quiz, just as there are no clear-cut boundaries for success. Only you can appraise what might be holding you back from realizing your potential—and how limitless a future you really want.

Whether we congratulate ourselves for it, or not, each woman knows how resourceful she has been, at certain times in her life. And (like the child, Orville Wright, who once daydreamed he could fly) you can devise your own ways to build your wings for soaring—and enjoy the thrill of a fresh beginning.

An Afterword from the Author

As you probably guessed, this book is not just about body energy; it is also about self-evolving. *Homo sapiens,* and the female sex, especially, can open up a higher order of being, once we learn to coordinate and use our bodies and minds to a greater degree.

To understand the exciting promise of this, consider your thumb. Use of the human thumb separates us from every other mammal and animal. Only we have learned ways to place the thumb in careful opposition to the forefinger. This makes possible the precision grip. It makes possible fine tuning of those electronic and mechanical devices that, due to this evolutionary development, only we could invent.

Today there is more gray matter within the human brain that is devoted to thumb manipulation than brain area used to regulate and control the abdomen and chest. Yet it was only after apes learned to walk erect that the hands were liberated. Once freed, hands—and the thumb—came to develop in more complex ways. With use, such movements etched new pathways in the brain and nervous system. Now one-third of the body's estimated five million sensory nerves are found in the hand.

Why haven't the rest of our bodies evolved more in recent centuries? Psychologist Stanley Keleman says our present civilization is a "disembodied" culture. Since Puritan and Victorian times we have been encouraged to think of ourselves primarily as mental beings—using the flesh as a container for our thoughts or an instrument to effect them. But (as we saw in the preceding chapters) a new page was turned in medical annals at the time of Wilhelm Reich, just a few decades ago. Scientists and psychologists are now hailing the body, itself, as a joyous way to open up enlightenment and self-realization.

Women, more than men, are brought up to be a bit reticent about our physical selves. Many of us were conditioned to feel that a woman's emotions make her weak, inferior and "unreliable." This is obsolete sexist thinking and medical male chauvinism.

Using "Bodypower" techniques, there are endless possibilities for the future of women. Because of our emotional responsiveness (rather than in spite of it), women can be the first to discover, shape and instruct our world in many powers that are still uncharted: the ability to heal, ESP, precognition, psychic communications and interplanetary thought transference. (Even *body* transference is not outside the realm of possibility for a highly evolved twenty-first-century woman!)

193

There is not a woman reading this book who cannot teach herself to outthink pain—and thus defuse and conquer it. Woman's perceptivity and insight could speed business and labor negotiations, as well as international diplomacy. New inventions and careers are as varied as the individuality of women, themselves.

For you, the reader, the real impact of our new "Bodypower" knowledge will come when you experience (perhaps for the first time in your life) the untapped resources of your own body. When a woman who has been shy or apologetic about herself first discovers the dependable reality of her own stamina, it is a kind of miracle. To be able, with surefire certainty, to make your body do what you want it to do builds confidence and pride. Like early joys of pregnancy (or simply being a woman) this must be experienced to be understood; it cannot be described by others.

To help you grasp the way that self-esteem relates to evolutionary development, let me tell two little stories. One is legend, the other is historical fact.

In Denmark, at Ladby, near the island of Fyn, a traveler can inspect a glass-enclosed, authentic Viking boat from the latter part of the eighth century. Of special interest are nearby descriptions of Viking funeral customs, such as those for which the Ladby vessel was used. We are told that when a Viking chieftain died, his body was placed in state. His pet dog, if any, was slain and placed in the boat at his feet. Then a night of drinking and revelry ensued. As a ritualistic part of this celebration, the widow of the Viking chief was summarily raped by each and every male member of the tribe. If she happened to live through this, she was killed outright—as a final gesture of sacrifice to her dead husband and domestic master.

In the archeologists' description, no word is added about what horror it must have been for the grieving widow to be stripped of her children and her dignity, then debased and mutilated with such nightmarish cruelty. No mention is made of why the other Viking women permitted such outrage to one of their own—eight hundred years after the beginning of our "modern" Christian era. (Perhaps Rousseau's words are the most accurate: Slaves lose everything in their chains, even the desire to escape them!)

Yet consider briefly these cowed, abused, hopeless women. Now think on those enlightened women in recent years who have changed the destiny of millions and guided nations with their own two hands: Margaret Sanger, Golda Meir, Indira Gandhi. To murmur that women have come a long way in the past thousand years is ludicrous understatement. The point of this book is—we can go still further. Let me illustrate this thought with a legend from the Orient. In that part of the world, emotional truths are more respected than in our fact-loving, pragmatic Western culture.

It is said that the gods were in a dilemma as to where to hide man's true divinity. One god said, "Put it at the bottom of the sea." "No," replied another god: "Man will learn to swim and walk underwater. Someday he will find it there." Another god said, "Put it atop the highest mountain; he will never find it there." Another replied, "No. Someday man will learn to make expert use of his climbing ability, and discover it." Finally, one god said, "I know. We will hide the divinity of man within his own body. The human is stubborn, and he will never think to look for it there." The other gods nodded agreement. And so man's divinity was hidden—within himself.

For many centuries, it has been a debate of theologians and Biblical scholars as to why Jesus of Galilee liked to employ a certain highly ambiguous title to describe himself. Rather than the terms *the Prince of Peace, the Savior,* or *the Heir of God,* the term He preferred to use was . . . *the Son of Man.* I would like to suggest that this was His way of dramatizing the spiritual promise of self-evolving. In a sense, He was agreeing with Gautama Buddha: *You, too, can become the Buddha.*

As you put into practice the body magic that this book can bring, save "space" within yourself for growing. When this joyful power comes to make a real difference in your life, as it has in mine, I'd love to hear about it. (A letter to me, in care of this publisher, will be forwarded.) Even if your first achievement seems minor (such as finally getting up the nerve to obtain a motorist's license), this eventually can bring enormous changes in your life. I shall rejoice and be pleased, along with you. For once a woman gets decisive about the small things, it becomes easier for her to tackle the large ones.

If you have enjoyed this book, I'll ask two favors: be a little kinder, today, to a stranger of your own sex; her burdens may be greater than you know. And telephone an old friend, perhaps one with whom you haven't spoken in years. (Friends drift apart for trivial reasons sometimes. We forget the wisdom of Euripides: *Woman is woman's natural ally.*)

Finally, dare to do something you didn't think you were quite up to doing. Only by trying and risking our talents regularly, by frequent outreach, can we develop into the super beings we are highly capable of becoming. The dancer Isadora Duncan turned a mediocre talent and a most ordinary appearance into an event-filled, colorful life. Her favorite quotation, from Nietzsche, was the one she constantly repeated to her students—"Be hard! Strive for the Infinite."

In like manner, I'd like to conclude my good wishes for your future with this thought from the French essayist-novelist André Gide: "If you love me, burn my books—and write books of your own!"

Marylou McKenna

For the Reader: Biorhythm Source List

1. To obtain a computerized biorhythm charting, personalized to your birth, write: Biorhythm Computers, Inc., 298 Fifth Avenue, New York, New York 10001. Six-months chart is $5.00, plus postage. A Do-It-Yourself Biorhythm Kit, including 12 chart blanks for charting friends (and lovers!), is $4.50, plus 35¢ postage, U.S.

2. Or write: Computerized Biorhythms, Inc., P.O. Box 229, East Orange, New Jersey 07019. A year's charting costs approximately $11. (Be sure to include your date and time of birth.)

3. Or the George Thommen book (included in our medical bibliography) features bio-engineered shortcuts. These help you chart biorhythms with precision.

How to Chart Your Biorhythms*

All you need are your birth date and some minor common sense. Let's say you were born on April 10, 1924.

First, figure the number of days you've lived from your birth date to your last birthday, April 10, 1972, by multiplying 365 times your age— 48 in this case. Then add a day for each leap year—12 in this hypothetical example.

* (Reprinted by permission: *Family Safety Magazine*, National Safety Council)

$$365 \times 48 = 17,520$$
Leap years $= \underline{\quad 12 \quad}$
17,532 days

Now let's assume today is July 6, 1972, which means you've lived 48 years plus 87 days, or a total of 17,619 days.

Now to compute your 23-day physical cycle, you simply divide the total days you've lived by 23:

$$\frac{766 \text{ "and 1 left over"}}{23 \,)\, 17,619}$$

Or, as of July 6, 1972, you've lived 766 23-day physical cycles plus one day.

Now get yourself some graph paper like that used in the accompanying illustration (or improvise your own). At the bottom, write in the 31 days of July, from left to right.

Again supposing that today is July 6, 1972, mark the number 6. On that day, you've lived through 766 complete 23-day physical cycles *plus one day*.

Now simply backtrack or subtract one day and, on July 5, therefore, you start a new 23-day physical cycle or rhythm.

So on July 5, you draw a 23-day curve, rising then falling above the median line, then—halfway or 11½ days later on July 16—it crosses the median line and zooms down, then up, once again intersecting the median or zero line on a new upward swing on July 28 (see illustration).

All of this means you'll experience "critical" days—physically—on July 5, July 16 and July 28.

For your 28-day sensitivity cycle and 33-day intellectual cycle, repeat for each by dividing your total number of days by 28 and 33, respectively. Then check your arithmetic with the curves below.

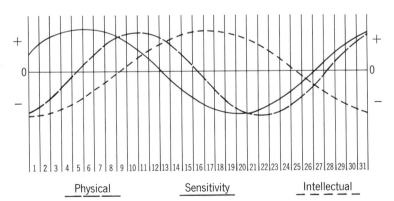

Physical   Sensitivity   Intellectual

Medical Bibliography

Abse, Dannie. *Medicine on Trial.* New York: Crown Publishers, 1969.

Alexander, F. Matthias. *The Resurrection of the Body.* Edited by Edward Maisel. New York: University Books, 1969.

Asimov, Isaac. *The Human Body: Its Structure and Operation.* Boston: Houghton Mifflin Company, 1963.

Baker, E. "Vitamin C and Stress." *American Journal of Clinical Nutrition* 20 (1967):583.

Barnes, W. "Variation in Energy Potential." *American Journal of Physiology* 207 (1964):1242.

Benarde, Melvin A. *The Chemicals We Eat.* New York: American Heritage Press, 1971.

Bergajo, P. "Postmenopausal Estrogen Therapy and Thrombosis." *Tidsskr Nor Laegeforen* 92 (December, 1972):2354.

Bieler, Henry G. *Food Is Your Best Medicine.* New York: Random House, 1965.

Bircher, Ruth. *Eating Your Way to Health.* Translated by Claire Lowenfeld. London: Faber and Faber, 1971.

Borek, Ernest. *Man, the Chemical Machine.* New York: Columbia University Press, 1952.

Boston Women's Health Book Collective. *Our Bodies, Ourselves.* 2nd rev. ed. New York: Simon and Schuster, 1976.

Brauer, Earle W. *Your Skin and Hair.* New York: The Macmillan Company, 1969.

Bromley, D. B. *The Psychology of Human Ageing.* Middlesex, England: Penguin Books, Ltd., 1966.

Brown, Roscoe C., Jr., and Kenyon, Gerald S. *Classical Studies on Physical Activity.* Englewood Cliffs, N.J.: Prentice-Hall, Inc., 1968.

Bruch, Hilde. *Eating Disorders: Obesity, Anorexia Nervosa and the Person Within.* New York: Basic Books, 1973.

———. "Conceptual Confusion in Eating Disorders." *Journal of Nervous and Mental Diseases* 133 (1961):46–54.

Burg, Alan W. "How Much Caffeine in the Cup?" *Tea & Coffee Trade Journal,* January, 1975.

Cannon, Walter B. *The Wisdom of the Body.* New York: W. W. Norton & Co., Inc., 1932.

Carpenter, Edmund. *They Became What They Beheld.* New York: E. P. Dutton, 1970.

Chafetz, Morris E., Blane, H. T., and Hill, M. J. *The Frontiers of Alcoholism.* New York: Science House, 1970.

Chesler, Phyllis. *Women and Madness.* New York: Doubleday & Co., Inc., 1972.

Clark, Marguerite. *Why So Tired?* New York: Duell, Sloan & Pearce, 1962.

Cohen, M. E., and White, Paul Dudley. "Life Situations, Emotions and Neuro-circulatory Asthenia (Anxiety Neurosis)." *Life Stress and Bodily Disease*, Vol. 29, *Proceedings of the Association for Research in Nervous and Mental Diseases*. Baltimore: Williams & Wilkins, 1950.

Cooper, Kenneth H. *Aerobics*. New York: M. Evans and Company Inc., 1968.

Cohn, C., and Joseph, D. "Changes in Body Composition Attendant on Force Feeding." *American Journal of Physiology*, 196 (1959) : 965.

Confessions of a Gynecologist. Garden City, N.Y.: Doubleday & Co., 1972.

Crescitelli F., and Taylor, C. "The Lactate Response to Exercise and its Relationship to Physical Fitness." *American Journal of Physiology*, 1967.

Dalrymple, Willard, and Diell, Harold S. *Healthful Living: A Textbook of Personal and Community Health*. New York: McGraw-Hill Book Company, 1973.

Danowski, T. S. *Sustained Weight Control: The Individual Approach*. Philadelphia: F. A. Davis Company, 1973.

Davis, Adelle. *Let's Eat Right to Keep Fit*. New York: Harcourt, Brace & World, Inc., 1954.

Day, Sister Agnita Claire (S.S.M.), Maygoski, Kathleen A., and Rubin, Marilyn B. "Postural Muscle Tremor Increased in Amplitude Following Cigarette Smoking." A research paper introduced at a meeting of the American Societies for Experimental Biology, April 10, 1974.

Devi, Intra. *Yoga for Americans*. Englewood Cliffs, N.J.: Prentice-Hall, Inc., 1959.

Dewan, E. M. "The P Hypothesis for Rems." *Psychophysiology* 4 (1968) : 365–66.

Diamond, Edward. "Can Exercise Improve Your Brain Power?" *Reader's Digest*, May, 1973.

DiCyan, Erwin. *Vitamins in Your Life*. New York: Simon and Schuster, 1974.

Dill, D. B., and Sactor, B. "Exercise and Oxygen Debt." *Journal of Sports Medicine and Physical Fitness*, 1966.

Dreiske, Paul. "Are There Strange Forces in Our Lives? *Family Safety Magazine*, Summer, 1972, pp. 14–23.

Drescher, Dennis G. "Noise-Induced Reduction of Inner Ear Microphonic Response." *Science Magazine*, July 19, 1974.

Feldenkrais, Moishe. *Awareness Through Movement*. New York: Harper & Row, 1972.

Feldman, Silvia. "Alexander Lowen: A Profile." *Human Behavior Magazine*, June, 1974.

Fishbein, Morris. *The Handy Home Medical Adviser and Consise Medical Encyclopedia.* New York: Doubleday & Company, 1963.

"A Fondness for Naps in Maoist China." *New York Times,* September 30, 1973.

Frankfort, Ellen. *Vaginal Politics.* New York: Quadrangle/The New York Times Book Co., 1972.

Fulton, John F. *A Textbook of Physiology.* Philadelphia: W. B. Saunders Company, 1955.

Galton, Lawrence. *The Silent Disease: Hypertension.* New York: Crown Publishers, Inc., 1973.

Goodman, Joseph I. *Diet and Live: A Guide to Corrective Eating.* New York: World Publishing Company, 1966.

Gray, Madeline. *The Changing Years.* Garden City, N.Y.: Doubleday & Co., 1967.

Gumpert, Martin. *You Are Younger than You Think.* New York: Duell, Sloan & Pearce, Inc., 1944.

Guthrie, Douglas. *A History of Medicine.* Philadelphia: J. B. Lippincott Company, 1946.

Hackett, Earle. *Blood: The Biology, Pathology and Mythology of the Body's Most Important Fluid.* New York: Saturday Review Press, 1973.

Hayward, J. "Hormones and the Aetiology of Breast Cancer." *Guy's Hospital Report* 121/1 (1972) :51–61. London: Breast Unit, Guy's Hospital.

Hilliard, Marion. *Women and Fatigue: A Woman Doctor's Answer.* Garden City, N.Y.: Doubleday & Co., Inc., 1960.

Hittleman, Richard L. *The Yoga Way to Figure and Facial Beauty.* New York: Hawthorn Books, 1968.

———. *Yoga: A 28-Day Exercise Plan.* New York: Workman Publishing Company, 1969.

Ho, Betty Yu-Lin. *A Chinese and Western Guide to Better Health and Longer Life.* New York: Pilot Books, 1974.

Hollingsworth, D. F., and Greaves, J. P. "Changes in the Pattern of Carbohydrate Consumption." *Proceedings of the Nutrition Society* 23 (1964) :136.

Hope, Bob. "How I Solved *My* Energy Crisis." *Family Health Magazine,* March, 1974.

Hoskins, R. G. *The Tides of Life: The Endocrine Glands in Bodily Adjustment.* New York: W. W. Norton & Co., Inc., 1933.

Hunt, Valerie V., and Massey, Wayne W. "Electromyographic Evaluation of Structural Integration Techniques." 1974. Unpublished scientific research data lent to author.

Jacobson, Edmund. *You Can Sleep Well.* London: Whittlesey House, 1938.

Janerich, D. T. "Hormones and Limb-Reduction Deformities." *Lancet,* 2 (July 14, 1973) :96–97.

Johnson, R. G. "Relative Importance of Inactivity and Overeating." *American Journal of Clinical Nutrition* 4 (1956) :37.

Jolliffe, Norman. *The Prudent Diet.* New York: Simon and Schuster, 1963.

Karlins, Marvin, and Andrews, Lewis M. *Biofeedback: Turning on the Power of Your Mind.* Philadelphia: J. B. Lippincott Co., 1972.

Kastenbaum, Robert. "Age: Getting There Ahead of Time." *Psychology Today,* December, 1971.

Kaufman, Sherwin A. *The Ageless Woman: Menopause, Hormones and the Quest for Youth."* Englewood Cliffs, N.J.: Prentice-Hall, Inc., 1967.

Kent, Patricia. *An American Woman and Alcohol.* New York: Holt, Rinehart & Winston, 1967.

Kraskin, Robert A. *You Can Improve Your Vision.* Garden City, N.Y.: Doubleday & Co., 1968.

Kraus, Hans. *Backache, Stress and Tension.* New York: Simon and Schuster, 1965.

Lear, Martha Weinman. "All the Warnings Gone Up in Smoke." *New York Times Magazine,* March 10, 1974.

Leis, H. P., Jr. "The Pill and the Breast." *N.Y. State Journal of Medicine* 23(1970) :2911–18.

Lesnick, G. J. "The Breast and the Pill." *N.Y. State Journal of Medicine* 17(1971) :2058–60.

Lewin, Roger. *Hormones: Chemical Communicators.* Garden City, N.Y.: Anchor Press/Doubleday, 1973.

Lewis, Howard R., and Lewis, Martha E. *Psychosomatics.* New York: The Viking Press, 1972.

Lilly, John C. *The Center of the Cyclone.* New York: The Julian Press, 1972.

Loebl, Suzanne. *Conception, Contraception: A New Look.* New York: McGraw-Hill Book Company, 1974.

Lowen, Alexander. *Depression and the Body.* New York: Coward, McCann & Geoghegan, Inc., 1972.

———. *The Betrayal of the Body.* New York: Macmillan Publishing Company, Inc., 1967.

Luce, Gay Gaer. *Body Time.* New York: Random House, 1972.

———, and Segal, Julius. *Sleep.* New York: Coward-McCann, Inc., 1966.

Maddison, D., and Viola, A. "The Health of Widows in the Year Following Bereavement." *Journal of Psychosomatic Research* 12 (1968): 297–98.

Mason, John W. "Confusion and Controversy in the Stress Field." *Journal of Human Stress*, Vol. 1 (March, 1975).

Mayer, Jean, *et al.* "Genetic, Traumatic and Environmental Factors in the Etiology of Obesity." *Physiological Review* 33 (1953) :472.

————. "Relation between Caloric Intake, Body Weight and Physical Work." *American Journal of Clinical Nutrition* 4 (1956) :169.

————. "The Physiological Basis of Obesity and Leanness." *Nutritional Abstract Review* 25 (1955) :597, 581.

McDowell, Bart, and Ward, Fred. "Those Successful Japanese." *National Geographic*, March, 1974.

McHenry, E. W. *Foods Without Fads: A Common Sense Guide to Nutrition.* Philadelphia: J. B. Lippincott Company, 1960.

McKenna, Marylou. *Revitalize Yourself: The Techniques of Staying Youthful.* New York: Hawthorn Books, 1972.

McQuade, Walter, and Aikman, Ann. *Stress: What It Is.* New York: E. P. Dutton & Co., 1974.

The Medicine Show. Compiled by the editors of *Consumer Reports.* New York: Pantheon Books, 1974.

Mellinkoff, Sherman M. "Chemical Intervention." *Scientific American,* September, 1973.

Miller, Neal E. "Decreased 'Hunger' but Increased Food Intake Resulting from Hypothalmic Lesions." *Science Magazine* 112 (1950): 256.

Mitchell, Helen S., *et al. Cooper's Nutrition in Health and Disease.* 15th ed. Philadelphia: J. B. Lippincott Company, 1968.

Montague, Joseph F. *How to Conquer Nervous Stomach Trouble.* Larchmont, N.Y.: Argonaut Books, 1964.

Morgan, Robin. *Sisterhood Is Powerful.* New York: Random House, 1970.

Naismith, Grace. "Antabuse Can Help Alcoholics." *Reader's Digest,* April, 1974.

Ostrander, Sheila, and Schroeder, Lynn. *Psychic Discoveries Behind the Iron Curtain.* Englewood Cliffs, N.J.: Prentice-Hall, Inc., 1970.

Palos, Stephan. *The Chinese Art of Healing.* New York: Bantam Books, 1971.

Pauling, Linus. "Orthomolecular Psychiatry." *Science Magazine,* April 19, 1968, pp. 265–71.

Perls, Frederick S. *Gestalt Therapy Verbatim.* Edited by John O. Stevens. Moab, Utah: Real People Press, 1969.

Pfeiffer, K., and Haake, K. "Mammacarcinom und Menopause." *Z. Alternsforsch* (Radiology College Publication) 14:3–4, pp. 307–313. Leipzig: Karl-Marx University, 1960.

"PGs Effective Postcoital Contraception in Animals." *Prostaglandin News,* Vol. 3, No. 3, the Upjohn Company newsletter, August 1974.

Pitts, Ferris N., Jr. "The Biochemistry of Anxiety." *Scientific American,* February, 1969.

————, and McClure, J. N. "Lactate Metabolism in Anxiety Neurosis." *New England Journal of Medicine* 277 (1967) :1329.

Recommended Dietary Allowances. 7th ed. National Research Council, National Academy of Sciences, Washington, D.C., 1968.

Richter, C. P. "Studies on Rats' Response to Stress." *Psychosomatic Medicine* 19 (1957):191.

Ring, F. O. "The Validity of Personality Profiles in Psychosomatic Medicine." *American Journal of Psychiatry,* 113 (1957):1075–1080.

Rubin, Theodore Isaac. *Forever Thin.* New York: Bernard Geis Associates, 1970.

Sadoff, L., *et al.* "Is Malignant Melanoma an Endocrine-Dependent Tumor?" *Oncology* 27 (1973) :244–57.

Sarkisov, S. A. *The Structure and Functions of the Brain.* Bloomington, Ind.: Indiana University Press, 1966.

Scarf, Maggie. "Oh, for a Decent Night's Sleep." *New York Times Magazine,* October 21, 1973.

Schachter, S. "Obesity and Eating: Internal and External Cues." *Science Magazine* 161 (1968):751.

————, and Gross, L. P. "Manipulated Time and Eating Behavior." *Journal of Social Psychology* 10 (1968):98.

Schutz, William C. *Here Comes Everybody: Bodymind and Encounter Culture.* New York: Harper & Row, 1971.

Selye, Hans. *The Stress of Life.* New York: McGraw-Hill Book Company, 1956.

————. *Stress Without Distress:* Philadelphia: J. B. Lippincott Company, 1974.

Singer, Charles, and Underwood, E. Ashworth. *A Short History of Medicine.* New York: Oxford University Press, Inc., 1962.

Silverberg, Gerald. "Unreasoning Radiation." *The Sciences* Vol. 13 (April, 1973). N.Y. Academy of Science.

Silverman, Julius. *Stress, Stimulus Intensity Control and the Structural Integration Technique.* A privately published research monograph, lent to this author.

Singh, Devendra. "Psychology of Obesity: Failure to Inhibit Responses." *Obesity and Bariatric Medicine,* September, 1974.

Solomon, Neil. *The Truth about Weight Control.* New York: Stein and Day, 1972.

Spark, Richard F. "Fat Americans: They Don't Know When They're Hungry; They Don't Know When They're Full." *New York Times Magazine,* January 6, 1974.

Stearn, Jess. *Yoga, Youth and Reincarnation.* New York: Doubleday and Co., 1965.

"Stilboestrol and Cancer." *British Medical Journal* 3:5775 (1971): 593–94.

Taylor, Eric. *Fitness after Forty.* New York: Arc Books, Inc., 1966.

Terhune, William B. *The Safe Way To Drink.* New York: William Morrow & Co., 1968.

Thommen, George S. *Is This Your Day? The Science of Biorhythm.* New York: Crown Publishers, Inc., 1973.

Thompson, Thomas. *Hearts.* New York: McCall Publishing Company, 1971.

Vaughan, Paul. *The Pill on Trial.* New York: Coward-McCann, Inc., 1970.

Vessey, M. P. "Oral Contraceptives and Breast Neoplasia: A Retrospective Study." *British Medical Journal* 3(Sept. 23, 1972):719–24.

Vitamin Information Bureau. *Calcium.* A 26-page monograph. New York, 1971.

———. *Iron.* A 21-page monograph. New York, 1974.

———. *Vitamin B-12.* A 22-page monograph. New York, 1972.

Watson, George. *Nutrition and Your Mind.* New York: Harper & Row, 1972.

Watson, Lyall. *Supernature.* London: Hodder and Stroughton, Ltd., 1973.

White, Kerr L. "Life and Death and Medicine." *Scientific American,* September, 1973.

Williams, Roger J. *Nutrition Against Disease: Environmental Prevention.* New York: Pitman Publishing Corp., 1971.

Winter, Ruth. *Poisons in Your Food.* New York: Crown Publishers, 1969.

Wynder, Ernest L., *et al.* "The Key Importance of Nutrition in Cancer Causation and Prevention." Research report introduced at the American Cardiology Society meeting, St. Augustine, Fla., March 22, 1974.

Yudkin, J., "The Practical Treatment of Obesity." *Proceedings of the Royal Society of Medicine* 58(1965):200.

Scientific Assemblies, Symposia and Television Documentaries

American Association for the Advancement of Science, 141st annual meeting, New York City, January 26–31, 1975.

Federation of American Societies for Experimental Biology, 58th Annual Meeting, Atlantic City, N.J., April 7–11, 1974.

"Focusing New Energies." Seminar sponsored by Esalen Institute and New York University, New York City, May 10–12, 1974.

"Nutrition and National Priorities." Seminar sponsored by Vitamin Information Bureau, New York City, Nov. 7, 1974.

"Perls and Rubenfeld." Private film previewed for author by Ilana Rubenfeld, former student of Dr. F. S. ("Fritz") Perls.

"Perls on Gestalt." Private tapes of Esalen Institute Gestalt Sessions conducted by the late Dr. Frederick S. Perls.

"Teen Age Alcoholism: The Bottle Babies." TV documentary, broadcast by WCBS, New York City, December 9, 1973.

"The Pursuit of Youth." TV documentary broadcast by NBC-TV, North America, May 30, 1974.

"Woman's Magazine." TV documentary first broadcast by WCBS, New York City, May 11, 1974.

Various Audio-Cassettes distributed to American gynecologists by Ayerst Laboratories, U.S. manufacturer of estrogen:—"Diagnosis and Management of Abnormal Bleeding in the Menopausal Patient." A talk by Dr. Robert B. Greenblatt, Professor and Chairman, Department of Endocrinology, Medical College of Georgia. *The Female Climacteric*, Vol. II, No. 2. (1973).—"Atrophic Vaginitis and Other Atrophic Changes in the Postmenopausal Patient." A talk by Dr. Robert W. Kistner, Assistant Professor of Obstetrics and Gynecology, Harvard Medical School. *The Female Climacteric*, Vol. I, No. 2. (1974).—"Management of the Principal Symptoms in the Menopausal Patient." A talk by Dr. Herbert S. Kupperman, Professor of Medicine, New York University Medical School. *The Female Climacteric*, Vol. I, No. 1. (1973).—"Sexual Dysfunction in the Postmenopausal Woman." A talk by Dr. William H. Masters, Director, Reproductive Biology Research Foundation, St. Louis. *The Female Climacteric*, Vol. II, No. 1. (1974).

All health statistics in this book are from the Metropolitan Life Insurance Company, New York, N.Y., the Division of Vital Statistics, U.S. National Center for Health Statistics, Washington, D.C., and the World Health Organization.

Index